IMAD'S

SYRIAN
KITCHEN

IMAD'S
SYRIAN
KITCHEN

**A LOVE LETTER
TO DAMASCUS**

BY IMAD ALARNAB

Interlink Books

FOUR

MAINS

136

FIVE

DESSERTS

200

SIX

DRINKS

236

IN SYRIA, THE SUMMER GOES ON for three months. It's always hot, every day. Blue skies and a perfect sun—you can count on it. I didn't pay attention to the weather when I lived in Syria, at all. Unless it was something special. But it was something special. It was so special. I realize that now. I didn't appreciate my bed until we had to shift from one place to another, sleeping on a two-seater couch or on the floor, or outside in the streets. But I appreciated it then. None of us fully appreciate what we have until it's taken away from us. We think it will stay like this forever, but I know now that it can all be lost.

In 2009, my biggest concern was where we would spend our next summer vacation. Or how we were going to celebrate my daughter's birthday, or where I was going to expand my restaurants to outside of Damascus. At that time, I ran three successful restaurants in Damascus, as well as juice bars and cafes around the city. I lived with my wife and three young daughters, with our family all around us. My children were doing well in school, we took trips to the countryside for picnics, we went to the movies or out to dinner with friends, we celebrated marriages and graduations and promotions at work. We were happy. Things were entirely normal and there was no way I thought that would ever change. But then, of course, everything changed.

WHAT IS A REFUGEE?

My name is Imad Alarnab, and I was a refugee, an asylum seeker, a displaced person, an illegal immigrant. What does that make you think of? Be honest. Does it make you think of people deciding one day to leave their home country for a more exciting job or better opportunities elsewhere? Do you think of smugglers helping people enter other countries in the backs of trucks and on overcrowded boats in the middle of the night? Do you think of thousands of people crashing onto coastlines all around the world to take advantage of the citizens and governments there? I made that journey from Syria to the UK that you've all heard about—on foot, on trains, with false ID, crammed into the back of cars, sleeping outside afraid for my life—and I can tell you, we are all just like you. We didn't choose to leave, it was not a decision any of us came to lightly. Every single one of us was forced. We had no choice. We fled our homes that we loved because we were no longer safe, or because our homes had been destroyed. Our families were in danger and we had to do what we could to keep them safe. What would you have done? We don't want to travel illegally. We don't want to take advantage of anything or anyone; we want to be part of a community, to work, to play our role in society again. We are all just like you.

On July 27, 2015, I hugged my family goodbye in Syria. Three months later I arrived in the UK, in October 2015. Leaving my wife and children behind, knowing the risks, was the hardest thing I've ever had to do. But I knew this was our only real chance at safety long term. My children were young, too young to make the journey with me; there were too many dangers ahead, too many unknowns. People often ask why I was intent on getting to the UK, why I wouldn't stop in Greece or Germany or somewhere else along the way. I had family in the UK, my sister, my aunt, and cousins, and I spoke the language already. Learning a new language is hard when you are older, and you need to speak it well to be able to work, and I wanted to work, I've always worked hard. Getting to the UK would mean my family could join me, we could all be safe, together again. I was scared about what might happen to me, but imagining the future if we stayed in Syria was even more terrifying.

When I left Syria, my eldest daughter was very emotional. She was frightened for me, and for herself and her sisters. She asked me to promise that we'd see each other within a year. And in that moment, I didn't know what else to do but to tell her "yes," even though I wasn't sure how or if this was even remotely possible. I didn't really even believe it myself. But on July 26, 2016 — a year to the day since I'd last seen them — I was hugging my family again, this time in the arrivals hall at London's Heathrow Airport. It was a surreal, unbelievable moment. Surely some kind of miracle. And then, in December 2022, six years later, we were granted our UK citizenship.

The journey to get here has been long, and often painful — both physically and mentally. It has been fraught with anxiety and many, many obstacles. I have lost people close to me, and I miss so much about my old life. But I know that the life I used to have is gone now, it simply isn't there anymore, and hasn't been for a long time. I am so, so lucky to have been given a new life here in London. The people of the UK have welcomed me, and I feel at home once again.

I am so proud of what I have achieved here. I am so proud of my restaurant, Imad's Syrian Kitchen, and of all the support and love people show it and me and my food. I want my journey to be looked upon as positive and encouraging for others, to show what can be achieved. But I also want people to know that it has not been an easy one. It's not only my story; it's for all of us who have had to leave our homes, who have been scared, who have struggled, who have felt alone and abandoned at times. I want to share my story so that people understand what we have all been through to get to where we are today. It's been very difficult, but as well as all the hatred and violence, I have been shown so much love. Having lost all faith in everything, I regained my belief in people during my journey, and I want everyone to know that. I want my story to reach as many people as possible. With the support of good people, with an honest heart, you can achieve incredible things.

FROM A CARWASH TO CARNABY STREET

As unlikely as it may sound, it was as a refugee stranded in Calais for sixty-four days that I started to find myself again. It sounds hard to believe, but that was the point at which I began to rediscover hope. We'd been donated a small hotplate, and I was able to cook. We'd pick up leftover ingredients from local cafes or supermarkets and I'd make meals for as many as 400 people a day! It gave us all comfort, and for me it was a taste of home, a reminder of who I was. It reignited my passion, gave

me purpose — and it gave me the courage to believe that things could improve. Cooking brings people together; it unites us all. And with the help of so many generous people, I've been lucky to be able to explore my love of food again, to share it with others. Honestly, nothing brings me more happiness than seeing people enjoying food I have cooked for them.

When I first arrived in the UK, I found work illegally in a carwash, getting cars ready to be sold. I slept there too, as an overnight security guard. I hated it. I hate cars! But I needed to work, to support myself and my family in Syria. I was a good salesman, though, and when I could work legally, I had a brief career selling the used cars I used to clean. But even though I was good at it, it wasn't where my heart lay. I thought about working in a restaurant instead, but even though I didn't love working at the garage, I knew I couldn't work in someone else's kitchen, cooking someone else's food or giving away my recipes. I did try at the very beginning. I went for an interview, but instead of seeing me cook or asking me about my experience, the owner asked me to empty and clean his van, then told me I didn't look like a chef and let me go. I went back to his restaurant after my pop-up had been featured in the newspapers and I saw in his eyes that he regretted it!

All throughout my life, but especially on my journey from Syria's warzone to my home in the UK today, I've been blessed by meeting the most amazing people, guardian angels looking out for me when I've needed them the most. How I came to open Imad's Syrian Kitchen starts with one of those angels, a woman called Toni. Once my family had joined me in 2016, we moved to a rented house in High Wycombe where we lived for a year. Toni was very active in supporting local communities, including assisting refugees, and she'd heard about a project called Cook for Syria, which helped raise money for UNICEF's Children in Syria Fund. She came to me and said, "I've been to your house, I've eaten your food, I know what you used to do back in Damascus. Would you like to be a part of Cook for Syria?" "YES!" Of course, I did. So, in January 2017, she introduced me to another amazing woman called Layla Yarjani and within a few weeks she'd started inviting people to my house for dinner. She'd call me and say, "There will be five people eating at your house in two days, will you be ready?" She introduced me to a PR company — still my PR company today — and from that moment on everything changed for me. Layla called me one day and asked "What are you doing on March 9th? You're running a pop-up restaurant in east London." Imad's Syrian Kitchen, the pop-up, ran for two weeks on Columbia Road, where the flower market is. All the ticketing and booking was organized, and the media contacted. A logo was designed. It was a dream come true.

The pop-up was supposed to be just a dinner each evening, but it was so popular that tickets sold out within 24 hours, and we ended up having two evening sittings and two Sunday lunches. I couldn't believe it. After that, I did pop-ups all over London, and catered for private dinners, weddings, and parties, here and in Ibiza, Paris, and Germany. But of course my ultimate dream was to have a permanent location, and in early 2020, Asma Khan — chef and owner of Darjeeling Express, who had become a friend during this time—told me about an available space on Carnaby Street. And, so, on May 19, 2021, Imad's Syrian Kitchen, the restaurant, opened its doors.

Nothing will compare to the feeling of that moment, of course—it was everything to me. It meant I had roots, that I belonged somewhere again. But cooking on the steps of a church in Calais, where I'd slept night after night, was where it had really all begun. The first stage of my new life. To cook for people was enough to remind me that this was the right path for me, it was what I was meant to do. I want to cook my food and make people happy. I forever want to hear people say that this is the best falafel they have ever eaten!

And that's what this book is for: to share my story, but also to share my recipes that have meant so much to me. Like me, they have traveled and evolved, influenced by what they have been through, adjusted and changed, but always staying true to their beginnings. These are the recipes I love, they are for you to enjoy as though I am making them for you in your home.

OUR NEW BEGINNING

When my family first came to the UK, my youngest daughter was six years old. In the car from the airport, her first question to me was how many police barriers there were between here and home. Her second question was how many hours of electricity do we have in the UK. And her third was for how many hours do we have water. I don't want my children to forget any of these things. I want them to appreciate what they have now, to know how lucky they are. But I also don't want them to be emotionally affected by what they have been through. I want their experiences to be encouraging and to inspire them to reach high for what they want to achieve, to have the confidence to follow their passions and realize their dreams. I don't want what they have been through to go on affecting them in the way it still affects me sometimes today.

Often, I wake up with a start in the middle of the night and say to myself, "Oh god, my mother will be so angry with me because I haven't spoken to her for so long!" and then I remember. When I heard she had died, I was living in a trailer on my own in west London. I had been in the UK for 50 days. I couldn't speak to her on the phone beforehand, or see her or go back to Syria to say goodbye. My Damascus died in 2012, and like my mother she'll never come back. I can dream about her, talk about her, think about her—but I'll never see her again in real life. And although I don't have closure over either my mother or my Damascus, I now have a new beginning for me, and for my family. I hope both my mother and my Damascus are looking down on me and are proud of me and of my daughters. I have fallen in love with London. London welcomed us in to be part of it, it made us feel at home, and I hope we will make London and its people proud too.

THE SYRIAN STORY SO FAR

In the winter of 2010, the Arab Spring began, first in Tunisia then elsewhere across the Middle East and North Africa. It was a long-awaited liberation for those countries, as their leaders who had held power, undemocratically for many years, were forced to step down by the demands of their people. A revolution was taking place and, in 2011, fifteen Syrian schoolboys, inspired by what they were seeing abroad, spraypainted on the walls outside their classroom: "The people want the fall of the regime." They were referring to the more than forty-year presidency of the Assad family. A regime that took from its own people and promoted its acquaintances, and yet still continued to achieve nearly 100 percent of the votes in "elections," their unrelinquishing rule passed down from father to son. It was a regime that hung over us all, with growing unemployment and economic hardships felt by many across the country. It was time for a change, for Syrians to take back their power.

It started as a peaceful revolution by a group of idealistic students, but it was supported by the people. All we wanted was justice, democracy. We even naively thought Assad would be on our side, that he'd step down, following what had happened in Egypt and Yemen. We thought he would listen to us. We thought the whole thing would be over within a few weeks. Maybe a few months. Definitely no longer than a year. Instead, those schoolboys were arrested and brutally tortured, and protests began against their treatment by the police. And then Assad started to use military force to bring an end to the uprising. But unrest had now spread across the country, other groups taking up the cause, and by 2012 there was a full-blown war happening all around us.

It affected everyone. We have all seen things we cannot unsee, and that will stay with us forever. At first, they happened at a distance — friends of friends, distant cousins on the other side of the city being caught up in gunfire, being injured, being imprisoned. Being killed. But then it came closer and closer until there was no escaping. This was no longer happening to other people; it was happening to all of us.

No one would ever have believed we'd be where we are now, twelve years on, with the situation worse than ever, with fighting between groups that aren't even Syrian: Russia, Iran, al-Qaeda, Turkey, the USA — Syria has become a place for battles to be played out that have nothing to do with its own people, and it looks like it's going to go on for a long time yet, with Assad's control even more extreme than before. All the people wanted was a voice. In a dictatorship, the people have no voice.

And now people are really, really scared. Friends have cut contact with me, blocked me on social media, because I have spoken out against Assad. The Syrian government, through the press, spread stories to divide the people, and they are now afraid for their lives for being a relative of or even for just knowing someone who says they are against Assad.

In January 2012, I was standing outside a mosque after prayers. People were shouting "freedom, justice," but it was calm, no aggression. Then from out of nowhere Assad forces descended and started shooting randomly into the crowd. Just three yards away from me, I saw a boy, no more than 13 or 14 years old, get shot in the chest. He died right in front of me. I was so shocked and afraid, I couldn't even look at him. No one could say or do anything. I knew then that there would be no justice in this revolution. There would be no closure.

Everyone has a story like that to tell, more than one. We see them when we close our eyes. When we think of a "home" that no longer exists for us.

Just a few weeks later, my eldest daughter was doing her homework in her bedroom. "I'm studying" were almost like the magic words she could say if she wanted to be alone. It was the secret password that meant no one could disturb her. My wife called to her to come into the kitchen. "I'm studying," came the reply. But this time my wife insisted and reluctantly my daughter joined her. Seconds later a bomb hit our apartment building. The whole side of the building where my daughter's bedroom was had been destroyed, with bricks and debris landing right on the bed where my daughter had been sitting. She would have been killed instantly. It's hard for me to think of that moment, even now. The shock, the relief, the fear of what could have been. The luck, the gratitude for whatever it was that made my wife persist. Even now we cannot talk about it together. We probably should, but it all feels too painful still.

We started shifting from one place to the next, as more and more areas became too dangerous to live in. Everyone's lives were now about survival, all while trying to hang on to as much normality as we could. But within just six days in 2012, all my businesses were destroyed and we had lost almost everything. But at least we were still alive.

In 2013, we were in a taxi heading to another new apartment in a safer part of Damascus. We were almost there when I got out of the car and headed away, back into the center of the city to look for work. I had been walking maybe five minutes when, from the exact direction in which the car with my family in had disappeared, I heard a huge explosion. It was an enormous bomb. Smoke and screaming came from where they were, and people were running away, terrified and crying. I found out later that 70 people had been killed. And in that moment, I was almost 100 percent certain my family was dead. I ran against the crowds, towards where the bomb had fell, dropping to my knees when I found the car and saw that everyone was OK. They were SO lucky to be alive, I almost couldn't believe it.

My wife hugged me close, down in the gutter, as we both took a moment to understand what had just happened. We then realized there were people that needed our help. The taxi driver took our children to safety, while we cleared the roads for the ambulances to get through and reached out to those around us in any way we could.

Around that time, I had a neighbor who worked for the Minister of Recollection, which was a department created by Assad to help end the revolution. (Its aim was to make it look as though people were coming together. Of course, in reality, it meant nothing.) And the Minister's security team was there too, helping in the aftermath of the bombing. After I had done all I thought I could do to help, I kissed my wife and began walking back into the city. On the way, I started noticing that people and policemen were shouting and pointing at me. They were shouting that *I* was the bomber. Because I had been seen running towards the bomb — towards my family — they thought I had been responsible.

The police grabbed me and started beating me right there in the street. No one did anything. They handcuffed me and drove me to Jisr-al Thawra (Revolution Bridge), which is one of the most corrupt police districts in Damascus, under a bridge. I was so scared; I thought I was going to be killed. No one asked me anything, not even why I had run towards the explosion in the first place. The Syrian police aren't interested in the truth, they just want to find someone they can hold up to say "they were responsible," so it looks like they've done their job. To execute someone. They kept beating me, so badly, kicking me, punching me, I was bleeding from my mouth. There was so much blood I was choking, so they turned me over, face down on the ground, and carried on. They were beating me so much that in that moment, I would have confessed just to make it stop. I would have confessed on TV if it meant this would end. That's how they operate.

But then the same security team who worked for the Minister came back: my neighbor. They shouted at the police that I wasn't the bomber, that I had helped rescue the injured, that they knew me, and that the Minister would be furious when he found out what had happened. I couldn't believe it; I had been saved. I often say that despite everything I've been through, I'm a really lucky person, and in that moment I believed it too.

I'm still suffering from what happened to me under that bridge, I feel the effects every day, in my body that won't let me try to forget, and in my mind.

KEY INGREDIENTS

These are the key ingredients to Syrian cooking. They are very helpful to have on hand in the pantry.

Most of my store-bought ingredients are Belazu brand. I find that Zaytoun do the best olive oil, za'atar, and dates. There is an online resource for special equipment named after a market in Damascus: www.ebay.com/str/almaskiya. You can find unusual ingredients in specialist stores or online, but most of these ingredients are available in the supermarket.

CHICKPEAS

Always start with dried for the creamiest hummus, not canned.

❖ ❖ ❖ ❖ ❖ ❖ ❖ ❖ ❖ ❖ ❖ ❖ ❖ ❖ ❖ ❖

DRIED MINT AND DRIED THYME

For drying mint, use fresh mint that is preferably not from a supermarket, as it will turn black. A plant grown outside will be perfect — the stalks are much thicker and better to use when they are dried, whereas the thinner stalks are better used fresh. Traditionally herbs would be dried in the sun and then crushed with your hands.

Wash the herbs well and then hang them up as a bunch, upside down, in the sun to dry. If you can't dry them in the sun, hang them somewhere warm, but remember that they will be breathing the air so it's best not done in the kitchen, instead use fresh air if you can.

After 2 – 3 days, they will be dried and crisp. Starting from the bottom and working your way up the stalks, rub the bunch between your hands to remove the crisp leaves; discard the stalks as they'll be too tough and chewy.

Store the leaves in an airtight jar, where they will keep for 6 months, although the intensity of flavor will lessen over time.

My mother used to put the dried herbs through a sieve to divide them, putting the very soft and fine herbs into a different jar. Use the fine herbs sprinkled over labneh, or in a sandwich, or onto buttered toast. The tougher, larger ones are used in cooking – famously used in tabakh roho (page 181) — or to infuse olive oil.

PINE NUTS

Pine nuts are usually toasted before use until golden brown so they hold their texture and add extra flavor. Toast in a small dry pan or in a baking sheet in the oven for 3 – 5 minutes at 350°F (180°C).

❖ ❖ ❖ ❖ ❖ ❖ ❖ ❖ ❖ ❖ ❖ ❖ ❖ ❖ ❖ ❖

POMEGRANATE MOLASSES

It took me ages to find the right one — not too sweet, the right consistency, good flavor — I use Belazu.

❖ ❖ ❖ ❖ ❖ ❖ ❖ ❖ ❖ ❖ ❖ ❖ ❖ ❖ ❖ ❖

RICE

We use many different types of rice. When we are going to stuff things, we use a short-grain rice that in Syria we call Egyptian rice. For topping it with something, like we're going to do with the kabsa (page 166), I like basmati or American golden rice, which is a slightly longer grain.

❖ ❖ ❖ ❖ ❖ ❖ ❖ ❖ ❖ ❖ ❖ ❖ ❖ ❖ ❖ ❖

TAMARIND

You can buy this semi-dried in 7 oz (200 g) packages — sometimes 14 oz (400 g). You can prep it all at once and keep in the fridge for up to 1 week, or just use as much as you need for the recipe. If you remember to do it the night before, great — just soak it in water first.

Crumble a 2⅔ oz (75 g) dried block into a saucepan with 1⅔ cups (400 ml) water. Over medium heat, bring it to a boil and boil it for at least 30 minutes to extract all the flavor and reduce the liquid. Strain through a sieve into a bowl; use a spoon to squash it through and scrape underneath into the bowl. You'll be left with about ¾ cup (180 ml) and it will have a really intense flavor. If you end up with a bit less than this, that's fine — it's all about the flavor.

THE WAY WE EAT

In some cultures, you eat with your hands or scoop up your food with bread. In others, people use spoons or knives and forks. Across Asia, it's chopsticks. In Syria, and especially in Damascus, we use it all. You can do whatever you like, eat however you want, because eating is your own personal comfort zone. It is the center of everything we do and there's no judgement, only enjoyment.

What is taken very seriously, though, are discussions about what you're going to eat next. It's a major topic! We never go anywhere without first deciding what food we will eat. Even going to the movies involves planning snacks. We might take grilled potatoes or Syrian-style pizzas; smaller, thinner, and crispier than Italian pizzas. After the movie, it's definitely a sandwich, eaten right next to the sandwich kiosk you bought it from. You don't go and find a seat, you have to stand and eat it right there, straight from the hands of the chef. And, of course, there has to be dessert.

In Syria, the weekends run Friday to Saturday, and for many years we went to my grandmother's house for brunch every Friday. The whole family would be there, and Syrian families are big! Cousins, aunts, uncles — it was like a huge party every week, and it was wonderful. Syrian families live close to each other, no more than half an hour away, and I remember those get-togethers as feeling part of something bigger, of being connected. It was important. It was always noisy, there was dancing, there was usually something to celebrate and, of course, at the center of it would be the food. There'd be a traditional fava bean salad served with pickles and yogurt, so delicious, dense, and heavy, you needed a nap afterwards! You can find the recipe on page 198.

Now that I'm living in the UK, our family time is on Sundays. We go on trips or just make time to spend with each other. And just like we used to do in Syria, we think about what food to take with us. It's never a sandwich bought from a service station, though! Can you imagine?! Damascus used to be surrounded by a beautiful countryside, with wide forests and rivers to explore, so much wildlife to enjoy. Of course, it's been ruined now by Assad, but before, we'd often head out there for the day or even to camp overnight. We'd buy fresh tomatoes, cucumbers, and parsley and we'd make a salad from scratch right there among nature. We'd fry summer vegetables: eggplants, cauliflowers, zucchinis. We'd pick berries for dessert. And there'd be a barbecue: lamb skewers, lamb fillet, lamb fat, all grilled on an open fire. Maybe some chicken too: with shish taouk, or chicken thighs like on page 155. A whole day spent outside in the fresh air, with food as its focal point.

18

Every activity, every outing, has certain foods associated with it, and this is a huge and exciting part of the planning. Even a trip to the hammam involves the question, who's bringing the mojadara and pickles?! But eating out isn't how we usually eat. In Syrian culture, almost all of our meals are cooked and shared at home. Just like in the west, though, it can be hard to get everyone together at the same time — with different schedules for work and school and other commitments — so most families try to eat at least one meal together each day, and traditionally it's lunch. Breakfast and dinner in Damascus are something light, maybe something with cheese or eggs. Dinner could be falafel or a sandwich eaten on the field after playing soccer. Lunch, though, is the main meal and there are always lots of plates on the table to share with everyone. To us, the idea of having just one plate of food is silly when there are so many textures and flavors to enjoy. We need more than one option!

In Syria, we say that the eye eats before the mouth, so even if it's a casual midweek meal, it needs to be colorful and well presented. There's always hummus and fresh breads, maybe a heavier meat dish or two, some vegetables or salads, and pickles. There's always more than we can all eat in one sitting, so there's always leftovers. Those leftovers then go back in the fridge and become tomorrow's meals, along with some freshly made extras, maybe a new salad or a rice dish, something hot, or a crunchy side. That's how we eat. We take what we already have and add to it, so even though we cook every night, it may only be a quick dish to supplement what's already there. And that is how the recipes in this book are meant to be enjoyed too. Make a few recipes, save what you don't eat for the next day, and add to it with one or two new dishes. It's why we make hummus in such large batches, so there's always some in the fridge!

Syrians show their love through cooking and, although we may keep our own family meals fairly simple, if you are a guest in a Syrian home you can expect something a whole lot more complicated. Spending three days preparing a meal is not unusual and symbolizes just how important you are to the host. The more difficult the dish, the richer and heavier it is, the longer it takes, the more respect we are showing you. It drives me a bit crazy! I'd rather spend quality time with my guests than be exhausted from cooking for days. But that's the Syrian way. My mother was very competitive about her cooking like this — she needed to be number one. If you happened to mention that someone else's cooking was nice, she'd then need to hear that hers was the best!

For us, there's no such thing as too much food. The recipe on page 117 makes a lot of falafel, but for Syrians, there's never more than you need. If you really can't eat all of what you have made, share some with your neighbors. In Damascus, we all lived closely together and this made us very sensitive to the people around us. If we're having a barbecue, we'd always send over a plate for our neighbors. And I do the same now I live in England!

If we're having lamb skewers, I'll share some over the fence — it's rude not to. And my neighbors now come over with whatever they have been cooking for me to try too — that's how I learned I loved gingerbread men!

I think one of the best things about Syrian food is that you can feel your way with it. You get to know the flavors you like, and you can make it your own. Of course, every Syrian thinks they know the correct way to make traditional dishes — and they definitely won't hold back in telling you. I honestly think it would make a Syrian unwell if they didn't give you their feedback about a dish! And that feedback is usually based around how their mother used to make it and why yours is wrong . . .

When I opened my first restaurant in Damascus, it was usual for a place to sell just one type of food — falafel or pizzas or burgers. But mine was bigger and we sold many different dishes. It gave me a chance to try something new. And then we opened a second and a third. I also ran a catering company, mostly cooking for non-Syrians on business trips to Damascus, which gave me the freedom and space to be even more experimental, as they didn't know what was traditional and what wasn't!

The recipes in this book are my recipes. They're mostly authentic, classic Syrian recipes, but in London I have the freedom to be a bit more creative, too. I'm not afraid to change things a little, and I've adjusted some of the recipes to suit how people here like to eat. My dishes may be a bit lighter, or sometimes I come up with entirely new dishes. For example, there's a dish called saroja on page 111. It's named after an area near where we lived in Damascus, which I loved and think of often, and this recipe reminds me of what it felt like to be in that place. Others are my mother's recipes that I've made my own, or they are the recipes I cooked along my journey to the UK that reminded me of who I was when I started to feel lost. It's food to bring people together.

So choose a few dishes you like the sound of and enjoy the process of creating a table of food, the Syrian way — really, anything goes! The dishes here are some of my favorites, but adapt them and do it your own way, and I can't wait to hear what you think.

ONE

SPICE
MIXES

ONE

SPICE MIXES

◆ DUKKAH 29   BAHARAT 32 ◆

KABSA SPICE MIX 32 ◆ RED TAOUK 33

◆ SHISH TAOUK 33 ◆ IMAD'S SAUCE 36 ◆

CILANTRO OIL 37 ◆ ORANGE-INFUSED OIL 37

SPICES

I THINK SPICES give different results depending on whether they are whole or ground. I prefer to use pre-ground spices and just mix them together, but if you want to grind your own, make sure you grind them very finely; I prefer to use a mortar and pestle rather than a spice grinder.

For all the mixes, combine the ingredients, transfer to an airtight container, and you can store them for use for up to 6 months.

DUKKAH

Every family has their own recipe for dukkah (literally "smashed" in Arabic), so feel free to create your own version. I haven't added any nuts and seeds to this, since I like to add them at the end when I'm ready to use it. The reason is that spices are drier than nuts, so they absorb the oil and moisture from the nuts and don't stay as crunchy and fresh.

MAKES 4 OZ (115 G)

½ cup (50 g) cumin seeds
1⅔ tablespoons coriander seeds
2 tablespoons pink peppercorns
3½ tablespoons Urfa chile flakes
1⅔ tablespoons Aleppo chile flakes

Toast the cumin and coriander seeds in a dry pan over high heat, stirring them around, until a little bit of smoke comes off. Take off the heat and add the pink peppercorns to toast in the residual heat for 30 seconds. While still hot, use a mortar and pestle to grind them, then tip into a small bowl. Stir in the Urfa and Aleppo chile flakes and, when cool, transfer to a jar and store for up to a month.

When you want to use the dukkah, toast any nuts and seeds you have on hand until golden (I like cashews and white sesame seeds), then crush with a mortar and pestle and add to the spice mix.

BAHARAT

Lebanese 7 spices

"Baharat" means mixed spices — seven spices. You can buy this ready made (or in a pinch you can substitute with garam masala) but if you want to make your own, here's how. It will keep in sealed jar for 6 months in a cool place.

Pictured on page 30.

MAKES A SMALL JAR

1 tablespoon ground black pepper
1 tablespoon ground cinnamon
1 tablespoon ground cardamom
1 tablespoon ground coriander
1 tablespoon ground cumin
½ tablespoon ground cloves
½ tablespoon ground nutmeg

Mix all of the spices together.

KABSA SPICE MIX

This is used a lot in Syrian cooking. It includes a lot of different spices but don't worry if you don't have them all. We use this spice mix but also use whole versions of these spices as they produce a different effect. It will keep in a sealed jar for 6 months in a cool place. You can buy this ready made if you don't want to make your own.

MAKES A SMALL JAR

1 tablespoon coriander seeds
1 tablespoon cumin seeds
1 tablespoon fennel seeds
1 tablespoon mustard seeds
1 dried black lime
1 bay leaf
1 tablespoon ground turmeric
1 tablespoon chile powder
1 tablespoon ground black pepper
½ tablespoon ground cardamom
1 tablespoon ground galangal
1 tablespoon ground cinnamon
1 tablespoon ground ginger
1 tablespoon mild curry powder

Grind the whole spice seeds with the black lime and bay leaf using a mortar and pestle or fine spice grinder, then combine with the ground spices.

RED TAOUK

This is a common spice mix that is used in many Syrian dishes.

MAKES A SMALL JAR

1 teaspoon sea salt
2 tablespoons paprika
½ tablespoon citric acid
1 tablespoon ground white pepper
1 tablespoon ground ginger
1 tablespoon chile powder
1 tablespoon ground cardamom

Mix all of the spices together.

SHISH TAOUK

You can buy this ready made, but I recommend making your own.

Pictured on page 31.

MAKES A SMALL JAR

1 tablespoon ground allspice
1 tablespoon ground cinnamon
1 teaspoon garlic powder
1 teaspoon ground nutmeg

Mix all of the spices together.

CONDIMENTS

IMAD'S SAUCE

Hot sauce

This is a great way to use up the last stray tomato in your fridge drawer.

Pictured on page 35.

MAKES A SMALL JAR

1 large, really red beefsteak tomato (or the best quality tomato you have), roughly chopped
1 green pepper, deseeded and roughly chopped
Small handful of mint leaves
½ teaspoon ground cumin
Juice of ½ lemon
1 garlic clove, roughly chopped
1 small red chile, roughly chopped
2 tablespoons good-quality extra virgin olive oil

Blend everything together in a blender until smooth. Season to taste and serve with anything—for example, kibbeh, hummus, falafel, etc.

CILANTRO OIL

Hot sauce

This will keep for up to 1 month.

Pictured on page 34.

MAKES 2 CUPS (500 ML)

2 cups (500 ml) good-quality extra virgin olive oil
1⅔ tablespoons cumin seeds
5 garlic cloves, very, very finely chopped
Large bunch of cilantro (3½ oz/100 g),
  including stems, chopped
Big pinch of salt

Add 1 tablespoon of the oil to a pan over medium-high heat, then add the cumin seeds, and cook until starting to pop. Add the garlic, cilantro, and salt then turn the heat off and add the remaining oil so that the cilantro leaves stay bright green. Allow to cool then transfer to a container.

ORANGE-INFUSED OIL

This will keep for 3–4 months
in a cool, dark place.

Pictured on page 39.

MAKES 4¼ CUPS (1 LITER)

3 large oranges
4¼ cups (1 liter) good-quality extra virgin olive oil

Pare the zest from the oranges using a swivel vegetable peeler, avoiding the white pith (if any comes off with the zest, slice it off with a knife).

Put the oil and pared zest in a heavy-based pot and bring to a very low simmer for 10 minutes. Be careful not to let the oil get too hot; we don't want to fry the orange zest — the trick is to make sure it isn't bubbling rapidly. If this starts to happen, remove from the heat for a minute to cool, then place back on the heat to continue.

Allow to cool, then remove the strips of zest and transfer to a jar or bottle.

TWO

BASICS

BASICS

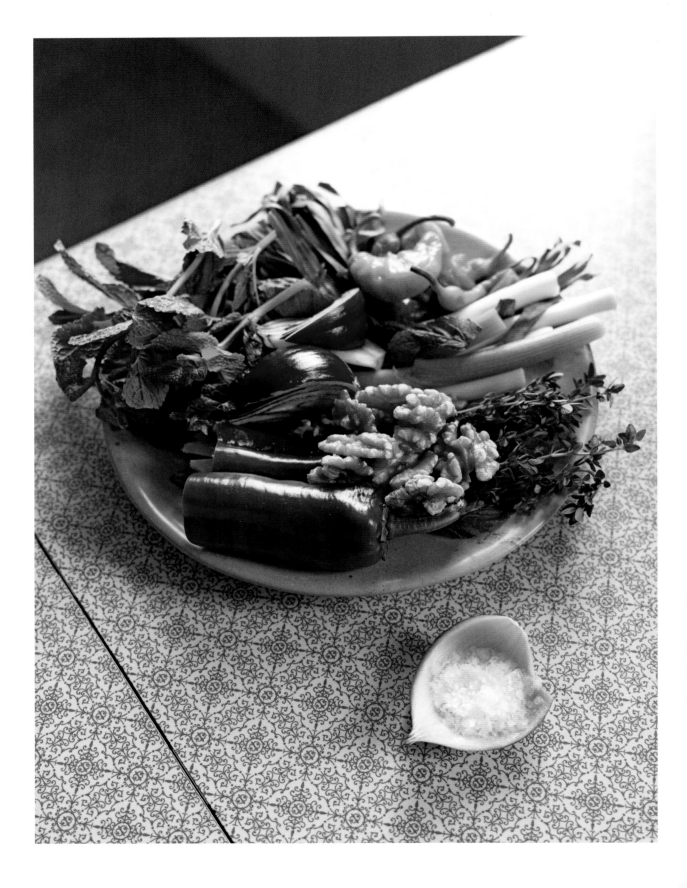

SAHAN KHUDRA

Green plate

There is something I love about Syria, which is "sahan khudra" — the green plate. I cannot think of this recipe without fresh mint, sliced Turkish green peppers — from the north of Syria — pickled cucumbers, radishes, fresh thyme, fresh lemon thyme, baby eggplant pickles, quartered small red onions. All of this can be used on the green plate. But you don't have to have it all at the same time.

It goes especially well with kebab hindi on page 144; instead of using a knife and fork to eat it, you use pita bread to scoop up the kebab and then eat with whatever you have from the green plate. Some people like to eat it with a slice of lemon, with the rind on. To go with kebab hindi, I would choose cucumber pickles and green pepper, using the green peppers as you would your fork, to scoop it all up.

The green plate will change completely if it's for breakfast; the combination mentioned above is for cooked meals only. At breakfast we'd have fresh cucumber, tomato, mint, thyme, and red onion, not green peppers or pickles.

HAWADIR

Ready things to present

In Syria, everyone is always ready to welcome guests at any time, and of course always with some food. In Damascus, we have something called hawadir, which means "ready things." So you have hawadir—jars of 2 or 3 types of olives, pickled eggplants, cheeses, cooked sliced beets in garlic oil, breads, and things to nibble on—on hand and ready to share at a moment's notice. In Syria, everything revolves around food and what you're eating next—even going to the movies. If you're visiting your parents, the first thing they'll think about is what they're going to feed you. It was a huge problem if I went to my mother's house and I didn't eat something! We don't visit each other when we're fasting; we visit to break our fast.

TO MAKE

✧ ✧ ✧ ✧ ✧ ✧ ✧ ✧ ✧ ✧ ✧ ✧ ✧ ✧ ✧ ✧ ✧ ✧

Jars of 2 or 3 types of olives
Pickled eggplants soaked
  in olive oil
Cooked, sliced beets
  in garlic olive oil

You don't need all of these for your hawadir, but we'd always have a good selection of these kicking around at home ready for the doorbell to ring.

RIZ SHAERIA

Plain rice

In Syria there is nothing called plain rice, or plain anything! We always add something to everything. In some countries, plain rice is just plain boiled rice, but in Syria rice is served with a lot of things — kebabs (page 144), tabakh roho (page 181), jaj bil furn (page 155), buttered halibut (page 170). We cook the rice with a very fine pasta, similar to angel hair pasta, and we always add spices. It would be too plain without it. We don't even consider salt and pepper seasoning; it's with everything. It's like waking up every morning. It's what you do next that's important.

TO MAKE

❖ ❖ ❖ ❖ ❖ ❖ ❖ ❖ ❖ ❖ ❖ ❖ ❖ ❖ ❖ ❖ ❖ ❖ ❖

1 cup (200 g) long-grain parboiled rice
2 tablespoons olive oil
½ teaspoon cumin seeds
1¾ oz (50 g) angel hair pasta or vermicelli, broken into short pieces (a handful or so)
½ teaspoon baharat (see page 32)
½ teaspoon ground black pepper
½ teaspoon salt
1 tablespoon ghee or olive oil

Wash the rice — always wash your rice. We have not even one recipe with sticky rice. We have a term — riz fal fal — which means that the lady of the house is very proud of their rice, with each grain separated from the others. To do this, the rice needs to be very clean and washed many times until the water is clear. Put your rice in a bowl and swish it through cold water, then drain it and wash it again two or three times. We do this for every recipe that uses rice.

Leave the rice to soak in a bowl of clean water until ready to cook, then drain.

Heat the olive oil in a pot over high heat and cook the cumin seeds for about 30 seconds, until they change color.

Keep stirring and add the pasta to cook for 3 – 5 minutes, until it has all turned the same golden brown. Turn down the heat slightly so the water doesn't splatter.

Add the drained rice on top and stir it once or twice — but not too much. Then add the baharat, pepper, and salt. Mix, then pour in cold water until it comes ¾ in (2 cm) above the rice. Turn the heat up and gently stir. Cook with a lid off for 2 minutes until the water is boiling, then turn down to the lowest heat and cook for 15 minutes with the lid on. Take off the heat and add the ghee or olive oil, then quickly put the lid back on and leave to rest for 5 – 10 minutes.

When you stir it through with a fork gently, it will be shiny and all the ladies will be bragging about the riz fal fal with all the grains separated and fluffy.

BURGHUL SHAERIA

Plain bulgur

Unlike rice, we don't wash bulgur — it is forbidden to wash bulgur! You just don't need to. Plain bulgur uses the same technique as plain rice but with more oil, as bulgur is a lot drier than rice.

TO MAKE

✤ ✤ ✤ ✤ ✤ ✤ ✤ ✤ ✤ ✤ ✤ ✤ ✤ ✤ ✤ ✤ ✤ ✤

3½ tablespoons olive oil

½ teaspoon cumin seeds

1¾ oz (50 g) angel hair pasta or vermicelli, broken into short pieces (a handful or so)

1⅓ cups (200 g) bulgur

½ teaspoon baharat (see page 32)

½ teaspoon black pepper

½ teaspoon salt

1 tablespoon ghee

Heat the olive oil in a medium pot over high heat and cook the cumin seeds for about 30 seconds, until they change color.

Keep stirring and add the pasta. Keep stirring and cook for 4 – 5 minutes, until it has all turned the same golden brown.

Add the bulgur on top and stir continuously for 3 minutes — you need to stir it more than you would rice as it is more likely to stick. Then stir in the baharat, pepper, and salt. If at any point you think it's drying out, add a little more oil.

When you've mixed in the spices, remove the pot from the heat and pour in enough cold water to cover the bulgur by 1½ in (4 cm). The pot will be very hot so be careful it doesn't splutter up.

Gently stir together and bring to a boil, uncovered, then turn the heat down to very low and cook with the lid on for 15 minutes.

Take off the heat and remove the lid, then spoon in the ghee. Put the lid back on and leave for 5 minutes before fluffing up and serving.

SHATTA

Chile sauce

TO MAKE

✦ ✦ ✦ ✦ ✦ ✦ ✦ ✦ ✦ ✦ ✦ ✦ ✦ ✦ ✦ ✦ ✦ ✦ ✦

5 Scotch bonnet or
  habanero chiles
1 small red onion
3 tablespoons olive oil
1 tablespoon dried mint
2 garlic cloves, peeled
1 x 14 oz (400 g) can of tomatoes
½ tablespoon dried thyme
Large pinch of salt

Remove the stalks from the chiles. Peel and roughly chop the onion into ¾ in (2 cm) chunks, or a similar size to the chiles.

Add the oil to a medium pot with the chiles and onions and fry over medium heat for 15–20 minutes, stirring regularly, until they are soft.

Tip into a blender, add the dried mint, garlic, canned tomatoes, thyme, and salt, and blend until smooth.

Allow to cool, then transfer to a container and store in the fridge for up to 7 days. If you want it to last longer, add a few tablespoons of olive oil to the top and cover tightly.

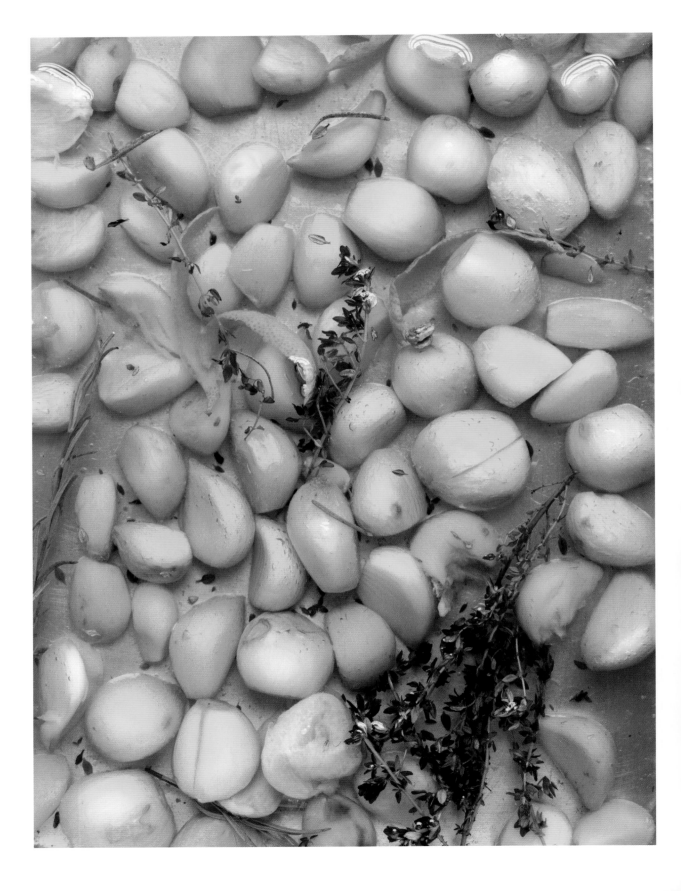

CONFIT GARLIC OIL

I serve this with everything, so use a good olive oil — the better the oil, the better it will taste.

I use this oil in my hummus as it gives it a sweet, mellow garlic flavor. You can also spread the soft garlic cloves on bread or toast with salt and pepper and chile flakes as snack, or pour the oil and garlic cloves onto labneh for your mezze.

I always have a jar of this in the house so I make a lot here, but you can halve the quantities if you don't want to make as much.

TO MAKE

✧ ✧ ✧ ✧ ✧ ✧ ✧ ✧ ✧ ✧ ✧ ✧ ✧ ✧ ✧ ✧ ✧ ✧

4 whole garlic heads, cloves separated and peeled
1⅔ cups (400 ml) your best extra virgin olive oil

Add the garlic to a small saucepan with the olive oil (they must all be covered, so add more oil if necessary) and place over the lowest possible heat — you don't want the garlic oil to boil (it should never reach 210°F/100°C). Cook very slowly for 10–15 minutes until the cloves are soft but do not take on any color. If the oil starts to bubble, remove the pan from the heat to cool a little, then place it back on.

(Alternatively, you can add all the garlic cloves with the oil to a small, wide roasting pan, again making sure the oil covers the garlic, then place in the oven at 320°F/160°C for 30–40 minutes until completely soft.)

Remove from the heat and let it cool completely before transferring to a jar. If the garlic is completely submerged in the oil, this will keep for up to 8 months in the fridge.

OPTIONAL EXTRAS

✧ ✧ ✧ ✧ ✧ ✧ ✧ ✧ ✧ ✧ ✧ ✧ ✧ ✧ ✧ ✧ ✧

Fresh thyme, rosemary, or bay
Pared lemon zest

TAHINI SAUCE

We use this for everything—a garnish,
dip, dressing; it's more like a seasoning
for us.

MAKES ABOUT 7 OZ (200 G)

¾ cup (200 g) tahini
Juice of 1 lemon
2 garlic cloves, smashed to a pulp
1 teaspoon salt
Ice-cold water

Mix together all the ingredients using either a hand
mixer or a blender on its lowest speed. It will be quite
thick, so add ice-cold water little by little until you
have a smooth, creamy sauce. It will keep, covered, in
the fridge for 5 days.

CRISPY ONIONS

These are a lovely addition to top
so many meals and add some crunch.

MAKES ABOUT 6½ OZ (180 G)

1 onion
1 cup (250 ml) vegetable oil
Pinch of salt

Halve and very finely slice the onion, preferably using
a mandoline, making sure the slices are all an even
thickness so they cook at the same rate.

Heat the oil in a heavy-based pot and add
the onion. Fry over medium-high heat for
5–10 minutes until very lightly golden. The trick
is to take them out a few seconds before they turn
a deep golden, as they will carry on cooking for a few
seconds after you remove them.

Using a slotted spoon, lift them out onto some paper
towels to absorb any excess oil, then allow to cool for a
few minutes to crisp up.

If they are not crispy enough, you can add them to
a baking sheet lined with parchment paper and toast
in the oven for 5–10 minutes at 400°F (200°C).

PICKLED CUCUMBERS AND CHILES

These purely sour pickles with no sugar, only salt, are very typical pickles from the Levant. It's really important to use the right salt here because the kosher salt draws out the moisture slowly, keeping the vegetables crunchy. Table salt is too fine, and will pickle too quickly and ruin the vegetables, and using regular coarse sea salt means they get soft and lose their crunch. If making in a different quantity, for every 4¼ cups (1 liter) of water you'll need 2 tablespoons of kosher salt.

TO MAKE

✧ ✧ ✧ ✧ ✧ ✧ ✧ ✧ ✧ ✧ ✧ ✧ ✧ ✧ ✧ ✧ ✧ ✧ ✧

8 – 10 baby cucumbers
2 tablespoons kosher salt
4¼ cups (1 liter) water
5 – 10 chiles
Peeled garlic cloves, as needed

Wash the cucumbers then slash 2 x ½ in (1 cm) vertical lines at the top and bottom of each, or any kind of slash, as this helps the pickling liquid to penetrate. Mix together the salt and water in a jug.

Place the cucumbers and chiles vertically in your chosen clear jar and press to fit in as many as you can. You want there to be as few gaps in the jar as possible; fill any large areas with garlic cloves.

Add the salty water until everything is completely covered, then close the jar very tightly with a lid. Put it in a dry, cool place out of the sun until the color has changed from bright green to a muted pickle green. In summer this will take 10 – 15 days but in winter it can take 15 – 25 days.

MY DAMASCUS

Damascus is one of the oldest cities in the world. Parts of it are thought to have been inhabited for as long as 10,000 years. And yet, for me, it doesn't exist anymore. It has become a fantasy, a memory, a dream, a fictional place that even if it were possible for me to board a flight to return there in safety, it wouldn't be there to welcome me back. My Damascus died in 2012.

I wish I could show everyone what my Damascus is. The people there have a pure heart, they are so generous. It has a warm feeling everywhere, even the walls feel warm. Everything glows. The walls are alive, listening, watching over us. You can feel kindness radiating out of the brickwork. When you say "hello," the people answer "tafadal"—welcome—and they mean it. If they ask how you are, you can't answer "I'm fine," you have to tell them really, what has happened since you were last in touch, how your family is, what they are doing. From your grandmother, this kind of detail is understandable, but these questions are from all your neighbors, the people you meet in the bakery, or when you're crossing the road. It can be a bit much! But we are also such an important part of each other's lives. We truly care about each other.

All Syrians are generous, but in Damascus they are very proud of their generosity. It makes our day if we make you smile. If you visited one of the markets, everyone would give you samples to taste, not because they want you to buy something, all they care about is making you happy and to hear "Wow! This is delicious." That's enough for them, there's no ulterior motive, no strategy.

In my neighborhood, Al-Qasaa, people from all religions—Jewish, Christian, Muslim, both Shia and Sunni—live together in amazing harmony. We celebrated Christmas with our Christian neighbors. We all honored each other's practices. Christian restaurants would paste newspaper over their windows during Muslim fasting times, and when Christians were fasting, we wouldn't have barbecues, so they couldn't smell delicious cooking over the walls. Ours was an especially mixed area, but all across the city we lived happily side by side, as we had for hundreds of years, and it was beautiful. Syrian men are family men, and we value our sons and daughters equally. Of course, you will always find macho men, but the respect we show to each other—to our elderly, to our women, how we care for one another—is something I love most about the Syrian people.

I've visited every big city in Syria, and most of the smaller ones, too. I've traveled from the border with Iraq to Turkey, from Lebanon to Jordan.

I love other cities in Syria, and have spent many beautiful times there — As-Suwayda and Al-Hasakah are high up there on my list of wonderful cities — but Damascus is my true love, my number one.

In Damascus, we deal with our food as though there is a love story between us. We use our hands to wrap our bread, and we take pride in preparing everything ourselves. Choosing to eat "organic" isn't a thing because everything is always organic. You don't need to go anywhere special to get it because you can see it growing naturally. Until just a few years ago, no one bought milk in plastic cartons; you'd take your own bottles with you to the people selling the milk directly and you'd fill them up. You'd buy eggs straight from the farmer who kept the chickens. Your vegetables were bought seasonally, even if this meant buying 50 kilos (110 pounds) of eggplants! And we'd freeze our own beans for the winter. We'd turn it into a family occasion. We'd gather around the table for a couple of hours with two big bowls in front of us: one full of beans to be podded and the other for the shiny green beans, carefully released from their pods. And then we'd eat green beans for a week and enjoy the rest months later when the snow fell. Fava beans, too. We'd chop our own tomatoes and store them in jars or in the freezer. Dried herbs as well, and spinach and another leafy green called mlukhea. It was a family ritual to pick the leaves from the stems and pack them into the freezer. All the families did this in Damascus. We all had a larder or pantry with wooden shelves, kept in perfect cool conditions so that our stores would last all year. We'd keep cheese there, too. The cows would produce so much milk in the summer, after having their calves, so we'd make cheese by boiling the milk for a long time and then preserving it ourselves.

Unfortunately, people don't tend to do much of this now. They don't trust the electricity, which can go off at any moment for who knows how long, so everything in the freezer or cool room would be ruined. And if you google images of Damascus, instead of those warm, blushing walls, you'll see buildings painted white, red, green, and black to show loyalty to Assad and the regime. Or just piles of rubble.

People often ask me if I miss Damascus, but it is Assad's Damascus now, not mine. There is electricity for one hour every twelve hours. There is no gas or diesel for people to travel, or to run the school buses. Schools are closed for two weeks over the holidays, not three days like before. In Syria, the weekend is now Friday, Saturday, and Sunday, and not because of any four-day relaxed working week. It's because the government cannot afford to fund the infrastructure, the transport network, the power to keep the office buildings running. But if you watch Syrian TV, they'll tell you life is good and Assad is great. They've been brainwashed or they're in denial, afraid for their lives. It's a broken country, a destroyed city.

It's been coming a long time, though, and maybe we were all in denial for too long. In my lifetime, we've never had any real ministers or elected government. That's not how it works in a dictatorship. In 1991, I had a car accident where a bus drove straight into me and I was in coma for 47 days. A medical police officer came to report on the accident and he told my family that the driver was now in jail. That there had been justice for what had happened to me. But then he recognized my uncle, who was also a doctor, and realized they had trained together. He said, "I'm going to tell you the truth." And the truth was that the driver was from the Soviet Union Embassy and he had returned to Russia the day after the accident, so no charges were brought against him. A free man. I'm still suffering from the effects of that car crash today. The revolution may have started in 2011 but the corruption has been going on far further into our history.

I can never go back. I am too afraid. I have been too outspoken against the regime, about Assad. There are Syrian army leaders on YouTube warning those who have left Syria not to return or else they will be killed. We are viewed as traitors. And I'm sure they are keeping track of what some of us are up to. When I had my pop-up in 2019, the Syrian media — Assad's propaganda machine — started talking about my empire of restaurants across Europe, achieved because I'd sold my soul to Western governments. They posted photos of me on social media. I didn't even have one restaurant! I wrote to them to ask why they were lying, but of course they didn't answer any of my messages.

Although I may not have any real closure on the death of my Damascus or my mother, I am lucky enough to have found a new beginning here in London — and I wish the same for Damascus too. I hope it will allow another young person, just like I was back then, to one day be able to have their own "my Damascus."

THREE

APPETIZERS, MEZZE & DIPS

APPETIZERS, MEZZE & DIPS

HUMMUS

This recipe makes a lot of hummus, but in Syria we like to always have hummus in the fridge. We make a big batch and eat it over 2 – 3 days at breakfast, lunch, dinner, and as a snack. We eat it all day with pita bread — and it's also great with chips and on the side of many dishes. There's pretty much nothing that hummus doesn't go with. It will keep, covered, in the fridge for up to 5 days, but if on day 4 you think it's lost a bit of its taste, you can lift it up with a little bit of tahini or cumin and it will be fresh again. If you don't want to make this much, feel free to halve all the quantities.

"Hummus" in Arabic literally means chickpeas, and it is a very traditional, simple recipe — carrot or beet hummus doesn't exist for us (and in my opinion shouldn't exist!). But what we do is add a lot of toppings — see page 70. The garnish is up to you, but the actual hummus itself is very simple. Although we are purists when it comes to hummus, I do have just a little twist in my recipe, to lift the flavors up.

I think one of the nicest things about making Syrian food is you can really feel it. There's nothing complicated in the recipes, so you can follow these or change them up and make them your own — it all depends on how you like them. I will give you a hint in these recipes, but I would love to see your creations using Syrian ingredients. It's not rocket science, you can feel your way — and feel love when you make them.

PREPARING THE CHICKPEAS

✧ ✧ ✧ ✧ ✧ ✧ ✧ ✧ ✧ ✧ ✧ ✧ ✧ ✧ ✧ ✧ ✧ ✧ ✧

2 ¾ cups (500 g) dried
  chickpeas
½ teaspoon baking soda

First you need to soak and then cook the chickpeas; all hummus (chickpea) recipes start this way.

Put the chickpeas in a large bowl and cover with cold water to twice their depth, with space above the water, too, for the chickpeas to expand. Leave to soak overnight or for at least 14 hours (but no more than 24, or the chickpeas will start to grow shoots), changing the water halfway through soaking.

Drain and rinse the chickpeas well then put them into a large pot. Cover with fresh cold water and bring to a boil. Boil for 10 minutes, then turn the heat down to a steady simmer. Now add the baking soda — be very careful when you add it as it will froth up. The baking soda makes the chickpeas evenly tender all the way through with no hard center, and also speeds up the cooking time.

How long you need to continue to boil the chickpeas depends on the kind you are using and their age. If you are using Mexican chickpeas, start checking on them at around 1 hour to 1 hour 15 minutes. To test, take a chickpea and smash it with your fingers: when ready, it should be really, really soft. This could take up to 2 hours.

FOR THE GARLIC OIL

✧ ✧ ✧ ✧ ✧ ✧ ✧ ✧ ✧ ✧ ✧ ✧ ✧ ✧ ✧ ✧ ✧ ✧ ✧

6 garlic cloves, peeled
Scant ½ cup (100 ml) olive oil

Meanwhile, put the garlic cloves in a small saucepan and cover with the olive oil. Bring to a low simmer, then turn down the heat and cook for 5 minutes until the garlic is a little bit brown and soft. Drain the garlic from the oil, reserving the oil and garlic separately.

FOR THE HUMMUS

✧ ✧ ✧ ✧ ✧ ✧ ✧ ✧ ✧ ✧ ✧ ✧ ✧ ✧ ✧ ✧ ✧ ✧ ✧

2 tablespoons ground cumin
1 tablespoon salt
3 tablespoons lemon juice
⅔ cup (160 g) tahini
⅔ cup (150 ml) water with
  4 cubes of ice added

If you like your hummus very smooth and creamy, you need to blend it while it's hot. I personally like it with some texture, so I drain the chickpeas, chill them in the fridge until cold, then start the blending process. You should have approximately 2 lb 4 oz (1 kg) cooked, drained chickpeas.

Put the chickpeas, 4 of the soft garlic cloves, and the cumin, salt, and lemon juice in a food processor and start blending. With the processor running, add the tahini — this will make it thicken up, so immediately add as much of the iced water as needed to achieve the consistency you like. I prefer to keep it a little bit liquid because when you put it in the fridge it will thicken up a bit by the next day.

Serve with a drizzle of the reserved garlic oil and the remaining 2 soft garlic cloves.

TOPPINGS

BOILED CHICKPEAS, SCALLIONS, CHILE FLAKES, AND PARSLEY

✧ ✧ ✧ ✧ ✧

Keep back a handful of the boiled chickpeas and toss them in a little of the garlic oil, along with a pinch of red chile flakes, a squeeze of lemon juice, a pinch of salt, 1 chopped scallion, and 1 tablespoon chopped parsley. Spoon your hummus onto a dish then scatter over the dressed chickpeas.

GARLIC OIL AND SUMAC

✧ ✧ ✧ ✧ ✧

You can use the garlic olive oil as it is, drizzled on top of the hummus, but at the restaurant we like to sprinkle a pinch of sumac on top, too.

SUMAC AND URFA

✧ ✧ ✧ ✧ ✧

Add a pinch each of sumac and Urfa chile flakes to the garlic oil with a squeeze of lemon juice. Mix together to make a dressing and drizzle over the top of the hummus.

HUMMUS BIL ZAYT

If you don't have time to soak and boil your own chickpeas for this, you can use 3 cups (500 g) drained jarred ones, which are a lot softer than canned ones. Simply reheat them in some boiling water for a few minutes. Use tomatoes that are seasonal — cherry tomatoes, beefsteak tomatoes, whatever is tasty at the time. Vine tomatoes are great.

1½ cups (250 g) dried chickpeas
Juice of 1 lemon
2 garlic cloves, smashed
  to a pulp or grated
1 teaspoon salt
1 tablespoon dukkah (page 29)
Bunch of parsley, chopped
2 scallions, chopped
2 medium tomatoes, diced
Scant ½ cup (100 ml) confit
  garlic oil (ideally; page 53) or
  extra virgin olive oil

Cook the chickpeas as directed on page 68.

In a small bowl, mix together the lemon juice, garlic, salt, and dukkah.

Put the drained chickpeas in a bowl while they are still hot, and toss in the lemon and garlic mixture. Top with the parsley, scallions, and tomatoes, and drizzle over the oil.

This also makes a really nice topping for hummus, if you have any left over.

VARIATION

HUMMUS BALEVAL (CHICKPEAS WITH YOGURT)

This is how my wife likes it. Mix together the lemon juice, garlic, salt, and dukkah as above. Then mix 3 tablespoons of Greek yogurt with 3 tablespoons of tahini, and add this to the chickpeas. Top with the parsley, scallions, tomatoes, and a drizzle of oil.

HUMMUS BIL LAHMA

There are many, many toppings for hummus in Damascus but this is the most famous.

2 tablespoons ghee
1 onion, finely diced
7 oz (200 g) ground lamb
1 teaspoon baharat (page 32)
⅓ cup (50 g) toasted pine nuts
Scant 1 cup (200 g) hummus
  (page 68)
Pinch of sumac
Small handful of parsley leaves
Salt and ground black pepper

Heat the ghee in a frying pan, add the onion, and fry until slightly softened, then add the ground lamb and baharat, with salt and pepper to taste. Cook, stirring, until the meat is soft and cooked through but not crispy, then add the pine nuts.

Spread the hummus out on a dish and tip the meat mixture over the hummus. Sprinkle with the sumac and parsley leaves and serve.

YLANGY

Vine leaves

This dish is great for any vegan friends you might be feeding. You can find vine leaves in jars in supermarkets. They will be rolled on top of each other but you can simply unroll them. Drain the vine leaves from the liquid and cut off the stems, then lay them out. If you have fresh vine leaves that is obviously better. You need to trim the stem, then dip them in boiling water that has a teaspoon of salt added. This makes them a little softer and easier to roll out.

FOR THE STUFFED VINE LEAVES

❖ ❖ ❖ ❖ ❖ ❖ ❖ ❖ ❖ ❖ ❖ ❖ ❖ ❖ ❖ ❖

1 cup (200 g) short-grain
  Egyptian rice
2 large beefsteak or vine
  tomatoes, very finely diced
1 red onion, very finely diced
1 tablespoon dried mint
2 teaspoons ground cumin
1 teaspoon baharat (page 32)
3½ tablespoons olive oil
50 vine leaves (see introduction)
Salt and ground black pepper

For the filling, wash the rice until the water runs clear then add to a bowl with the tomatoes, red onion, dried mint, cumin, baharat, olive oil, and a good pinch each of salt and black pepper, then mix thoroughly.

Prepare your vine leaves (see introduction) then lay one out, ideally on a tray, in front of you. Spoon 1 tablespoon of the rice mixture into the middle of the leaf. Fold the sides inwards like an envelope, then roll away from you, making a neat little roll. Set aside on another tray and continue with the rest until you have used all the leaves and filling.

FOR THE SAUCE

❖ ❖ ❖ ❖ ❖ ❖ ❖ ❖ ❖ ❖ ❖ ❖ ❖ ❖ ❖

Juice of 4 lemons
2 cups (500 ml) water
1 tablespoon tomato paste
5 garlic cloves, smashed into
  a paste
1 teaspoon ground black pepper
1 teaspoon baharat (page 32)
¼ cup (60 ml) pomegranate
  molasses
2 teaspoons salt

Put the lemon juice and water in another bowl, then stir in the tomato paste, garlic, black pepper, baharat, pomegranate molasses, and salt, and mix together until combined.

76 **APPETIZERS, MEZZE & DIPS**

TO ASSEMBLE

✤ ✤ ✤ ✤ ✤ ✤ ✤ ✤ ✤ ✤ ✤ ✤ ✤ ✤ ✤ ✤ ✤ ✤ ✤

2 starchy potatoes, peeled
and cut into ½ in (1 cm) slices

In a wide, heavy-based pot or Dutch oven, about 12 in (30 cm) in diameter, layer the sliced potatoes to completely cover the base. Now stack the stuffed vine leaves neatly and tightly around the edges of the pot until you have used them all and have no big gaps.

Place a weight on top of everything. I have a traditional weight that is meant for this dish, but if you don't, then stack 3–5 plates on top instead, which works fine.

Pour over the sauce to cover everything; you might not need all of it, so just set aside the rest in case you need to top it up later. Tightly cover with foil or a lid then place over high heat until the liquid is boiling. Boil for 10 minutes then turn the heat to low and simmer for 1 hour.

Remove the lid and allow to cool completely, then serve as a side or main.

SAWDA

Lamb's liver

FOR THE LIVER

✦ ✦ ✦ ✦ ✦ ✦ ✦ ✦ ✦ ✦ ✦ ✦ ✦ ✦ ✦ ✦

1 lb 2 oz (500 g) lamb's liver, cleaned (and trimmed if necessary)
4 garlic cloves, peeled
1 green chile
2 tablespoons olive oil
1 tablespoon dukkah (page 29)
Scant ½ cup (100 ml) vegetable oil
1 red onion, thinly sliced
1 green pepper, deseeded and thinly sliced

Slice the liver lengthways into long slices ½ in (1 cm) thick.

Smash together the garlic, chile, olive oil, and dukkah using a mortar and pestle until you have a paste, then add half of this to the lamb liver in a bowl. Leave to marinate for 1 hour.

Heat the vegetable oil in a wok or frying pan over high heat. Once the oil is hot, add the liver and stir immediately. Keep stirring for 5–6 minutes until cooked through and golden. Now add the red onion and green pepper and stir to cook for 2 minutes. Drain off the excess oil/liquid then add the remaining half of the garlic and dukkah paste. Mix together then serve scooped up in flatbreads or pita, with tahini, parsley, pickles, and a squeeze of lemon juice.

TO SERVE

✦ ✦ ✦ ✦ ✦ ✦ ✦ ✦ ✦ ✦ ✦ ✦ ✦ ✦ ✦ ✦

Flatbreads or pita bread
2–3 tablespoons tahini
Small handful of parsley
Pickled cucumbers (page 56)
½ lemon, for squeezing over

FAMILY

FOR SYRIANS, family is a big deal — and it's also very big! My father was one of 14 brothers and sisters and the last time anyone counted, we had 98 immediate cousins. Whenever we all got together, it was always noisy, chaotic, and lots of fun. My family is so extended that it's actually almost impossible to keep track of everyone, especially now with so many having left Syria, dispersed around the world. Last year, a delivery guy came to the restaurant to drop off a package. He told me he was also Syrian, from Damascus, and that he had left with his parents to escape Assad. While we chatted about our shared experiences, he happened to mention his family name and we soon discovered that we were cousins! And not even distant cousins; his mother was my aunt. This is how vast and widespread Syrian families are, and also how we can never escape each other for long!

Family is a very important part of Syrian culture, maybe even more important than the food we eat! Before the war when so many of us fled the country, we lived close to each other, almost next door. And we made seeing each other and spending time together a priority. I'd see my mother several times a week, and I'd call her every day if I didn't see her. Syrians respect their elders. It's not from a sense of duty, we just genuinely want to look after those generations that have struggled through before us, that have given us so much. And it's not just those we are related to, either; we call all those older than us Uncle or Auntie as a sign of our affection. Never Mr. — that would be so formal, it'd actually be impolite. My daughters call my neighbor here Uncle David!

Now that we're living in the UK, of course it's harder to stay in touch with everyone and to maintain those relationships as much as we'd all like. We have our phones and Facebook, but it's dangerous for those still in Syria to be in contact with me, so they try to keep their distance. It's sad, but I don't blame them at all. Fear of the regime is everywhere and you cannot be too careful. If I even sent money to them, even just $50, they could end up in jail. It's illegal to receive foreign currency and the authorities would see it as showing loyalty to ISIS. They're just looking for reasons to arrest you, or make you disappear.

Living in the UK means my direct family around me is much smaller. My sister and her family live in Doncaster, and my dad mostly lives with them too. We see them as often as we can, but most of the time it's just me, my wife, and my three daughters. To me, my daughters are my everything. They are my greatest achievement, the light of my life. I wake up every day for them. If I hear the sound of them laughing, or if one of them hugs me or tells me they like something I have cooked for them, it feels like I don't need anything else in the world. Dana, Lana, and Mariam; I honestly can't describe how much I love them. They are the most incredible, intelligent, and well-behaved young women — but I really don't care if they are good or not. After all we've been through, all I want is for them to be happy. I know now that nothing is ever certain, you can't trust anything to stay the same. Our happiness when we are together as a family is our constant now. That is all that matters.

People say I talk about my daughters too much, but one of the reasons I love them so much is because they are my wife's daughters. Batool: absolutely, my better half. The love of my life who calms me down, supports me, keeps me going when I feel lost. There are hundreds of reasons why I love her; she is the most amazing woman. We have been married for more than twenty years, but I feel just as young as we were back then when we're together. My mother introduced us. She invited me to a family gathering and I had the feeling she was going to try to hook me up with someone there. I wasn't interested. I wanted to find a partner by myself, not be introduced to one of my aunt's friends! I went to the party entirely to prove her wrong and was set on not liking this person at all. But the minute I saw Batool, I knew that I had lost whatever game I was trying to play. I swear, I knew it in that instant. It felt as though we'd known each other forever. We were so relaxed with each other, as though we were already married. It was an incredibly strange and new feeling.

Of course, one of the reasons I love to cook is because it connects me to all this. All these memories, all that history, that culture, of my family, of the people around us, all mixed into the flavors, stirred deep into every dish. How each person likes something a certain way: less spice, more yogurt, their favorite fresh herbs. It's the same wherever you go around the world: secret family recipes passed down, recreating how your mother used to cook your childhood meals, the traditions and rituals you want to pass to your own children. It's where we originate from; it's our past and it's also the future.

When you sleep on the ground, when you are frightened for your life, when you go through tough times, you have a different relationship with your family. It makes you appreciate all your loved ones so much more. But I hope you don't have to go through what I have to love your family as much as I do. Just start loving them now.

KHUBZ

Flatbread

I demoed this on the BBC's *Saturday Kitchen*, so you can have a look on the website if you need visual help on how to make them. I always like to make extra so I can use them for recipes like fattoush on page 107.

TO MAKE

❖ ❖ ❖ ❖ ❖ ❖ ❖ ❖ ❖ ❖ ❖ ❖ ❖ ❖ ❖ ❖ ❖ ❖

4 ¾ cups (570 g) white bread flour, plus extra for dusting

1 teaspoon salt

1 teaspoon sugar

1 tablespoon fast-acting instant yeast

1 ⅔ cups (400 ml) lukewarm water

Mix together the flour, salt, sugar, and yeast in the bowl of an electric stand mixer, or a large bowl.

Gradually pour in the water and mix again, or tip out onto a floured surface and knead to a soft, nonsticky dough (4 – 6 minutes in a stand mixer or 8 minutes by hand). Cover and leave to rest for 30 – 60 minutes until doubled in size (the time will differ depending on how warm your house is).

Knock the rested dough back into the bowl then tip onto a floured surface and divide into 12 – 14 balls, each about the size of a golf ball. Cover with a tea towel and rest again for another 30 minutes.

Using a rolling pin, roll the balls out into circles ⅛ – ¼ in (5 mm) thick.

Heat a wok upside down over medium-high heat and spray with water. Place one of the pieces of dough on the upturned wok and cook for 30 seconds, then flip and cook on the other side for 20 seconds more. You can just do this in a frying pan if you prefer. Remove and wrap in a damp tea towel while you repeat with the remaining dough, spraying the wok with water between each one.

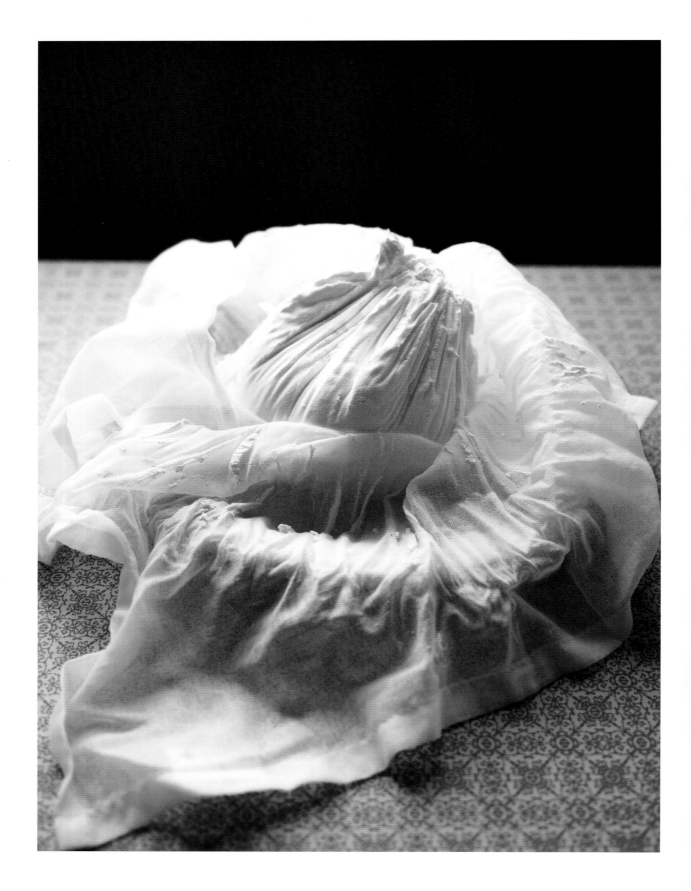

LABNEH

This makes a lot of labneh but it can last up to 10 days in the fridge. I've given the original, basic recipe below but if you want some extra flavor, you can add any herbs you want, either as you make it or later on before serving. We mix 2 tablespoons dried mint and 1 tablespoon dried thyme into the yogurt to make the labneh we have on the menu at the restaurant. In Syria we don't add a squeeze of lemon, but I wanted to do this in this recipe because the yogurt in the west is slightly sweeter.

You can treat this just as you would any soft cheese — spread it on toast or pita, or eat it in the morning with za'atar, olives, and a drizzle of olive oil. A favorite addition is okra deep-fried in cilantro oil (page 37), topped with fresh cilantro and Aleppo or other red chile flakes.

TO MAKE

✧ ✧ ✧ ✧ ✧ ✧ ✧ ✧ ✧ ✧ ✧ ✧ ✧ ✧ ✧ ✧ ✧ ✧

2 lb 4 oz (1 kg) Greek-style yogurt
Small squeeze of lemon juice (¼ lemon)
1 teaspoon salt

Mix the yogurt, lemon juice, and salt together very well, then put in a strainer to drain — we have dedicated strainers for this, but you can put the yogurt in a clean, dry tea towel in a colander set over a bowl. Place in the fridge to drain for 12 hours, then transfer the drained yogurt to an airtight container and keep in the fridge.

TOO MUCH?

✧ ✧ ✧ ✧ ✧ ✧ ✧ ✧ ✧ ✧ ✧ ✧ ✧ ✧ ✧ ✧ ✧ ✧

If you really think you have too much, there are lots of ways to use it up. One of the best ways is to turn it into *labneh mudabaleh*.

Line a tray with a clean, dry tea towel and spread the labneh from the recipe above on top. Keep it in the fridge for 2 days to dry it out further. Roll the dried labneh into balls. If you like you can now roll it in sumac, za'atar, dried mint, or any other flavoring. Store in a sterilized jar, covered in olive oil, and it will keep for several months in the fridge.

MTAFAYT BAMYEH

Okra and labneh

TO MAKE

❖ ❖ ❖ ❖ ❖ ❖ ❖ ❖ ❖ ❖ ❖ ❖ ❖ ❖ ❖ ❖ ❖ ❖ ❖

9 oz (250 g) okra
2 tablespoons olive oil
¼ cup (60 ml) cilantro oil
   (page 37)
Small pinch of sumac
Small pinch of Aleppo
   chile flakes
Scant 1 cup (200 g) labneh
   (see page 87 for homemade)

Wash the okra, trim the stalks off the ends, and dry in a clean tea towel. Then thinly slice into long strips.

Heat the olive oil in a pan and, once the oil is hot, add the okra and fry on all sides for about 5 minutes until golden and still crunchy.

Remove from the pan and put in a large bowl. Add the cilantro oil, sumac, and chile flakes and toss to coat.

Dollop the labneh onto a serving plate, then top with the okra. Finish by pouring over the remaining cilantro oil from the bowl.

Serve immediately.

BABA GANOUSH

Small eggplants are no good here; you need large ones. It's up to you how you char them — at the restaurant we do it over a flame, but you can also do it in the oven; I've given both methods below. You can top the baba ganoush with anything from the toppings list below, or just have it on its own.

Pictured overleaf.

TO MAKE

✧ ✧ ✧ ✧ ✧ ✧ ✧ ✧ ✧ ✧ ✧ ✧ ✧ ✧ ✧ ✧ ✧

3 large eggplants
Juice of 1 lemon
4 confit garlic cloves (page 53)
1 teaspoon ground cumin
1 teaspoon salt
Scant ½ cup (100 g) tahini
Olive oil, to drizzle (optional, see below)

Starting at the stalk, use a sharp knife to score lengthways from top to bottom all the way around on both sides of each eggplant. Don't go too far into the eggplant — about ¼ in (5 mm). This will make it easier when you come to scoop out the soft, cooked flesh.

If you're charring the eggplants in the oven, preheat the oven to 470°F (240°C), then place in the oven on a baking sheet for 30 minutes, turning them over as they cook. If you're charring them over a flame (either on your burner or on a barbecue), hold them carefully with tongs and keep turning them over. You're looking for the skins to be really blackened and charred, and the eggplant to almost collapse. Each eggplant has its own shape, size, and water content, but you can check inside the score line; when it is dark brown just inside, that means the middle is done. Remove from the heat and leave to cool a little.

When you can hold it with your fingers, split each eggplant in half and, keeping one half of each still in its skin, scoop out the flesh of the other halves into a food processor (discarding the skins on these halves). Add the reserved eggplant halves — including the skin — to the food processor with the lemon juice, garlic, cumin, and salt, and process until semi-smooth. The charred skin adds a really intense smoky flavor. Mix in the tahini, then serve with a stack of flatbreads, drizzled with olive oil or with one of the topping suggestions opposite.

Alternatively, you can finely chop the ingredients instead of processing, for a chunkier result.

TOPPINGS

✦ ✦ ✦ ✦ ✦ ✦ ✦ ✦ ✦ ✦ ✦ ✦ ✦ ✦ ✦ ✦ ✦

- Tahini sauce (page 54), drizzled over the top
- Pomegranate molasses, pomegranate seeds, and a drizzle of olive oil
- Chopped cherry tomatoes and olive oil
- Chopped rosemary
- Chopped parsley (we usually add this on top of any extra topping we use)

My very favorite topping — Shred 2–3 scallions into ¼ in (5 mm) strips. Fry with 2 crushed garlic cloves in 3½ tablespoons extra virgin olive oil. Add a pinch of salt. We often like to add a little chopped rosemary on top as well.

MUHAMMARA

If you can find them, use Romano (long) peppers here as the skins aren't as tough as on bell peppers. If you can't get hold of them, use bell peppers, but after roasting, add them to a bowl, immediately cover with plastic, and allow to cool. You'll then be able to easily peel off the tough charred skins.

TO MAKE

✧ ✧ ✧ ✧ ✧ ✧ ✧ ✧ ✧ ✧ ✧ ✧ ✧ ✧ ✧ ✧ ✧ ✧

5 red Romano peppers
2 red chiles
⅔ cup (75 g) walnut pieces
¼ cup (60 ml) red pepper paste
1 teaspoon ground coriander
1 teaspoon ground cumin
½ teaspoon salt

Preheat the oven to 425°F (220°C). Place the peppers and chiles on a large baking sheet in a single layer and roast for 20–25 minutes, turning halfway through, until the skin is blackened and charred on both sides. Allow to cool slightly then pull off the stems from each pepper and chile.

Spread the walnuts out on another baking sheet and toast in the oven for 5 minutes. Remove and allow to cool.

Put the chiles, red pepper paste, and spices in a food processor and blend to a paste. Now add the roasted peppers, walnuts, and salt and pulse carefully until you have a rough, chunky consistency. You don't want a smooth paste here.

TO SERVE

✧ ✧ ✧ ✧ ✧ ✧ ✧ ✧ ✧ ✧ ✧ ✧ ✧ ✧ ✧ ✧ ✧ ✧

2 tablespoons pomegranate
  molasses
Small bunch of parsley,
  finely chopped
½ red onion, finely chopped
Handful of pomegranate seeds
Extra virgin olive oil, to drizzle

Spoon into a bowl or onto a plate and drizzle with the pomegranate molasses. Garnish with parsley, red onion, pomegranate seeds, and a drizzle of olive oil.

LABAN

Yogurt

MAKES 8½ CUPS (2 LITERS)

8½ cups (2 liters) best-quality whole milk
¼ cup (60 ml) 10-day-old homemade yogurt

Bring the milk to a boil in a large pot. Take off the heat then transfer to a ceramic or clay heatproof container or a pot that ideally isn't clear. Let it cool until you can put your finger in it comfortably with it still being hot (roughly 115–120°F/45–50°C if you have a thermometer).

Add the yogurt and mix until combined. Cover with a tea towel or large cloth then wrap it all up in a blanket or large piece of thick fabric and place in a cool, dry place out of the sun for at least 12 hours.

Remove the blanket or fabric and cloth and put in the fridge, uncovered, for another 12 hours.

Keep it in the fridge and use the last few tablespoons to repeat the process, or make labneh or labneh mudabaleh (see page 87).

LABAN BI KHIAR

Yogurt salad

Yogurt should be naturally sour but some brands you get taste sweet. So get the best-quality sour yogurt if you can find it. This is often served with dishes like mujadara (page 158), kabsa rice (pages 162–166), or makloubeh (page 186).

MAKES 14 OZ (400 G)

½ cucumber
1½ cups (350 g) Greek-style yogurt or
    homemade yogurt (see left)
2 garlic cloves, finely grated or smashed to a paste
2 tablespoons dried mint
Good pinch of sea salt flakes
Juice of ½ lemon (optional)

Grate the cucumber into a mixing bowl and add the yogurt, garlic, dried mint, and salt, and mix together. If your yogurt is sweet, add the lemon juice to taste.

MY MOTHER

MY MOTHER WAS LIKE my Damascus: generous, hardworking, and overflowing with love for everyone around her. And also like my Damascus, she died without me being able to properly say goodbye, without being able to get that closure. But that doesn't mean I don't love them both still. I dream of them both, I speak of them both, but I know I will never see either of them in my life again.

I owe everything to my mother. Every single thing I do or think or say has been influenced by her. My cooking, my recipes, my lips, my short fingers! That I am able to speak English. Even the décor at the restaurant is inspired by the things she loved: the plants and pots and collections she kept in her home. I see something of my mother in each of my daughters, and it makes me love them even more.

I don't talk about my father much because I look so much like him. He used to tell me that he wanted me to be a better version of him. I think in life the only people you can genuinely say you want to do better than you, with true happiness, are your own children. As the eldest son, when I was six or seven years old, my father would take me to show me around the family business, to see what I would inherit one day, what I would become. This was my path. Almost my entire family was in textiles — uncles, aunts, cousins. It was what we did. The natural career for me was fashion designing — and I loved it! I did it for a long time, before I found my way into food. In Syria, you have to do military service when you are 18, but even as a kid I was never interested in playing with guns. So, instead, I went to Dubai to study fashion and even set up my own design studio. Here I was, 20 or 21 with a successful fashion business. But in my heart I knew it wasn't for me.

I set up my first restaurant in 2000 and it was a huge moment for my mother. She was the one who had taught me to cook, who had taught me everything I knew about food. The rest of the family were working in fashion or designing, but I had chosen restaurants and cooking. Somehow, my mother felt like she had won, and she was very, very proud.

My mother was the most brilliant person, full of joy. I wanted her to see the world more, to experience life more, but her happiness came from being creative, from being productive. She wove rugs, drew on glass, and painted on silk. I designed a dark blue jacket and she embroidered gold thread on top, and it was the most beautiful thing I'd ever seen. She was so creative, always searching for something new.

She had the most beautiful smile. She was truly radiant because she was comfortable in herself. She had an inner peace. She knew how to encourage others to be the best they could be, and she would always find a way to help. If someone was struggling, she'd be there for them. She tutored English and math, and loved to work with the totally lost causes, those who everyone thought had no hope! She had her own special way of explaining things and you could listen to her for hours. She not only taught me cooking, she taught me how to be a better person. She taught me more things than I can ever understand, than I will every fully appreciate — not to be selfish, but to help others, to be kind. I have a wonderful relationship with my wife and my daughters, I think mostly because of her. She used to take care of everyone around her, her family, her neighbors. Everyone loved her. When I left Syria, I couldn't bear leaving my wife and children behind, but she eased my anxiety, because I knew she'd look after them too.

Although she lived a relatively short life, it was a full life. If she was alive now, I honestly think my life would be so much easier. I could just ask her, rather than wondering, "what would Mama do?" I know it's futile, but a big part of me thinks about how I would love her to see me now, to talk to her about what I'm doing. I think she would have loved it, seeing people coming together to enjoy Syrian food, my recipes, her recipes living on.

My mother passed away when I had been in the UK just 50 days. I was alone and she was unwell in the hospital. Two days before she died, I asked my aunt to let me speak with her because I had this feeling it might be the last time. But my aunt told me to stop talking in that way, that she would be fine, not to start worrying everyone. My wife, Batool, was with her just before she passed, and says my mother opened her eyes and said to her: "Tell Imad I love him, and that I am pleased with him. He has my approval."

TABBOULEH

The key to this lies with the lemon, black pepper, and parsley. It's supposed to be sour and fresh to break the richness of a main dish; we would never order this on its own.

TO MAKE

❖ ❖ ❖ ❖ ❖ ❖ ❖ ❖ ❖ ❖ ❖ ❖ ❖ ❖ ❖ ❖ ❖

½ cup (100 g) fine bulgur
2 unwaxed lemons
Good pinch of salt
1 teaspoon ground black pepper
2 – 3 big bunches of parsley,
  very finely chopped
1 little gem lettuce, very finely
  chopped, plus leaves to serve
3 tomatoes, deseeded and
  finely diced
1 small red onion, finely diced

In a large bowl, wash the bulgur in cold water, then drain and place back in the bowl with enough fresh water to just cover it. Squeeze in the juice from 1½ of the lemons and set aside to soak for 1 hour. If after soaking there is excess liquid, drain before using.

Add the salt and black pepper and mix with a fork to separate the grains. Very finely chop the remaining half lemon (with its peel) and add to the bulgur, along with the parsley, lettuce, tomatoes, and red onion. Mix everything together well.

TO SERVE

❖ ❖ ❖ ❖ ❖ ❖ ❖ ❖ ❖ ❖ ❖ ❖ ❖ ❖ ❖ ❖ ❖

Handful of pomegranate seeds
Lemon slices
Extra virgin olive oil

Arrange a few lettuce leaves in a bowl and spoon in the tabbouleh. Serve topped with pomegranate seeds, some lemon slices, and a drizzle of olive oil.

JIRJIR

Arugula salad

TO MAKE

❖ ❖ ❖ ❖ ❖ ❖ ❖ ❖ ❖ ❖ ❖ ❖ ❖ ❖ ❖ ❖ ❖

Grated zest and juice of 1 lemon

3 tablespoons extra virgin
olive oil

1 tablespoon za'atar

1 teaspoon sumac

9 oz (250 g) halloumi,
cut into ¾ in (2 cm) cubes

3 handfuls of arugula leaves

14 oz (400 g) watermelon,
cut into ¾ in (2 cm) cubes

In a bowl, combine the lemon zest and juice, oil, za'atar, and sumac
and mix well. Add the halloumi and toss well to combine.

Place the arugula and watermelon on a large platter, followed by the
dressed halloumi. You can toss everything together or just serve as is.

SALAD VARIATIONS

BIWAS

This is a very flavorful salad, which is very refreshing to the tastebuds.

SERVES 4 AS A SIDE

1 large red onion, thinly sliced
Large handful of parsley, finely chopped
3 tablespoons pomegranate molasses
Juice of ½ lemon
Pinch of salt
Pinch of sumac

Mix all the ingredients together in a bowl.

DAGA

A famous dish in Palestine, this very traditional Syrian salad can be served with fish. It is refreshing and zesty.

SERVES 4 AS A SIDE

2 garlic cloves
Pinch of salt
1 green chile, sliced
2 ripe vine tomatoes, diced
4 scallions, chopped
Handful of parsley, roughly chopped
1 tablespoon extra virgin olive oil
Juice of 1 lemon

Very finely chop the garlic with the pinch of salt. Alternatively, mash them together using a mortar and pestle.

Place in a bowl with the chile, tomatoes, scallions, and parsley, then mix through the olive oil and lemon juice and serve.

CHERMOULA

This is full of fresh herbs, but thanks to the oil this will keep well in the fridge in an airtight container.

SERVES 4 AS A SIDE

Small handful of cilantro
Small handful of parsley
2 garlic cloves
1 preserved lemon
1 tablespoon capers
Scant ½ cup (100 ml) extra virgin olive oil
¼ teaspoon ground coriander
¼ teaspoon ground cumin
Grated zest and juice of ½ lemon
Salt

Finely chop the cilantro and parsley leaves and stalks, the garlic, preserved lemon, and capers, and add them to a bowl with the oil, ground coriander, cumin, lemon zest and juice, and a pinch of salt, or to taste. Mix to combine. Alternatively, add everything to a blender and pulse until semi-smooth.

This will keep, covered, in the fridge, for up to a week.

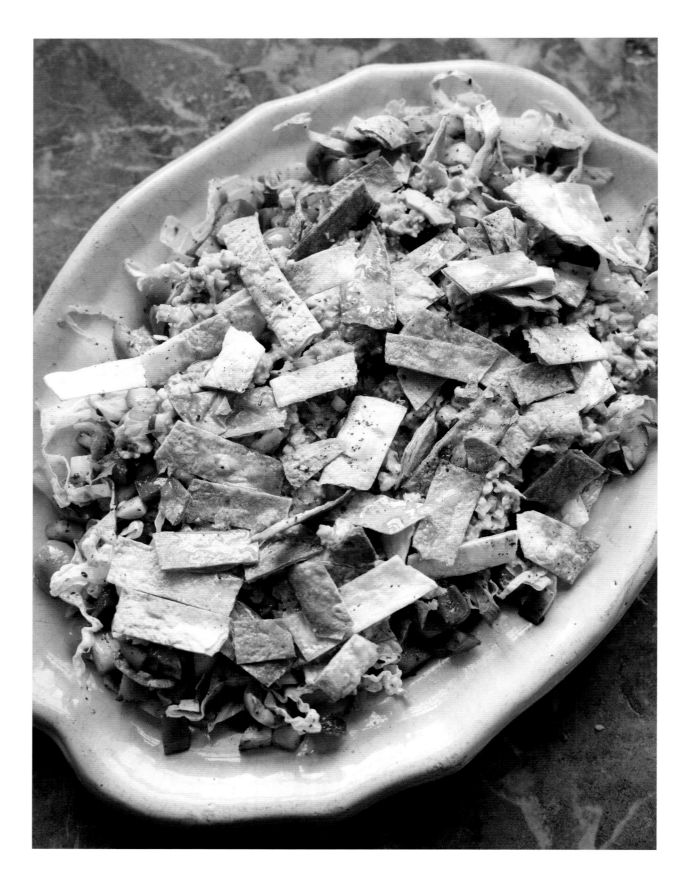

FATTOUSH SALAD

TO MAKE THE FATTOUSH

✧ ✧ ✧ ✧ ✧ ✧ ✧ ✧ ✧ ✧ ✧ ✧ ✧ ✧ ✧ ✧ ✧ ✧ ✧

½ teaspoon sumac
½ teaspoon dried thyme
½ teaspoon dried oregano
Small pinch of salt
1 tablespoon olive oil
1 thin flatbread (see page 82 for homemade) or flour tortilla, cut into thin strips

Preheat the oven to 400°F (200°C).

Mix together the sumac, thyme, oregano, salt, and olive oil and toss through the flatbread strips to coat them. Place them on a baking sheet in a single layer and toast in the oven for 5 minutes until crisp and golden.

FOR THE DRESSING

✧ ✧ ✧ ✧ ✧ ✧ ✧ ✧ ✧ ✧ ✧ ✧ ✧ ✧ ✧ ✧ ✧

2 tablespoons extra virgin olive oil
1 tablespoon apple cider vinegar
½ tablespoon pomegranate molasses
1 teaspoon sumac

Put all the dressing ingredients in a jar and shake to combine.

FOR THE SMASHED AVOCADO

✧ ✧ ✧ ✧ ✧ ✧ ✧ ✧ ✧ ✧ ✧ ✧ ✧ ✧ ✧ ✧ ✧

1 avocado, peeled and pitted
½ red onion, very finely diced
Juice of ½ lemon
½ red chile, finely diced (optional)

Mix all the smashed avocado ingredients together in a bowl, mash with a fork until smooth, then set aside.

FOR THE SALAD

✧ ✧ ✧ ✧ ✧ ✧ ✧ ✧ ✧ ✧ ✧ ✧ ✧ ✧ ✧ ✧

1 Romaine lettuce, finely sliced
3½ oz (100 g) vine or beefsteak tomatoes, cut into ½ in (1 cm) cubes
Scant ½ cup (100 g) pomegranate seeds
3 Lebanese or Persian cucumbers, cut into ½ in (1 cm) cubes
1½ oz (40 g) green olives, pitted and torn
Orange-infused oil (optional; page 37), to serve

Toss the salad ingredients together with the dressing. Top with the smashed avocado, followed by the toasted flatbread, then finish with the orange oil, if using.

SAROJA

Baby eggplants and cheese

Saroja is a neighborhood in Damascus close to where I lived, and this dish always reminds me of there.

FOR THE VEGETABLES

❖ ❖ ❖ ❖ ❖ ❖ ❖ ❖ ❖ ❖ ❖ ❖ ❖ ❖ ❖ ❖ ❖

12 oz (350 g) baby eggplants
1¾ cups (90 g) panko
  breadcrumbs
2 eggs
1 tablespoon za'atar
1 teaspoon salt
½ teaspoon ground cumin
A few grinds of black pepper
Small handful of parsley,
  finely chopped
Olive oil, for drizzling

Preheat the oven to 400°F (200°C).

Remove the stems from the eggplants and slice each in half lengthways, then slice each half across into half-moons ½ in (1 cm) thick. Add the slices to a bowl of salty water while you prepare the breadcrumb mixture.

Get 2 medium bowls and put the breadcrumbs in one and the eggs in the other. Beat the eggs well with the za'atar, salt, cumin, black pepper, and parsley.

Drain the eggplants and pat dry with paper towels.

Line a large, low-sided baking pan with parchment paper, then dip each eggplant slice into the egg mixture, followed by the breadcrumbs, making sure they are all evenly coated. Place the breaded eggplant slices on the lined baking pan.

Drizzle each slice with a little olive oil then bake in the oven for 20 minutes.

FOR THE CHEESE

❖ ❖ ❖ ❖ ❖ ❖ ❖ ❖ ❖ ❖ ❖ ❖ ❖ ❖ ❖ ❖ ❖

3½ oz (100 g) feta, crumbled
3½ oz (100 g) halloumi, grated
1 teaspoon black sesame seeds
1 teaspoon toasted white
  sesame seeds
¼ cup (60 ml) date molasses
2 tablespoons sour cherry molasses
Small handful of mint leaves,
  chopped

Put the feta, halloumi, and all the sesame seeds in a bowl and mix to combine.

In a separate small bowl, stir together the date and sour cherry molasses.

To serve, add the cheese mixture to a platter or plates and top with the crispy eggplant. Drizzle over the molasses dressing and finish with the chopped mint.

SABANAGH KHUDRA

Green spinach

TO MAKE

✧ ✧ ✧ ✧ ✧ ✧ ✧ ✧ ✧ ✧ ✧ ✧ ✧ ✧ ✧ ✧ ✧

1 lb 12 oz (800 g) large-leaf
   spinach
3½ tablespoons extra virgin
   olive oil
1 red onion, finely chopped
1 teaspoon ground black pepper
3 garlic cloves, smashed to a pulp
Handful of cilantro, chopped
2 tablespoons pomegranate
   molasses
Handful of pomegranate seeds
Good pinch of sea salt flakes
Cooked rice, to serve

Start by thoroughly washing the spinach in a large colander,
in batches if you need to. Remove any large, tough central stems,
then roughly tear and set aside.

Put the oil in a large pot over medium-high heat, then add the
red onion and black pepper and cook for 3–4 minutes until just
softened. Now add the garlic and cilantro and cook for a minute
before adding the spinach. Depending on what type of spinach you
have, it will take 1–3 minutes to wilt, so keep stirring it until just
cooked but still bright green.

Transfer to a serving plate and top with the pomegranate molasses,
pomegranate seeds, and sea salt flakes. Serve alongside cooked rice.

MTUMA

Crushed new potatoes

TO MAKE

✦ ✦ ✦ ✦ ✦ ✦ ✦ ✦ ✦ ✦ ✦ ✦ ✦ ✦ ✦ ✦

2 lb 4 oz (1 kg) new potatoes or
  fingerlings
¼ cup (60 ml) extra virgin
  olive oil
2 garlic cloves, crushed
3½ tablespoons salted butter
Salt and ground black pepper

Preheat the oven to 400°F (200°C).

Boil the potatoes in a large pot of salted water for 8 – 10 minutes
until soft. Drain, then allow to steam for a few minutes.

Put the potatoes in a large, low-sided roasting pan with 3 tablespoons
of the olive oil and a good pinch each of salt and pepper. Crush each
potato lightly by pressing down on them with the bottom of a glass,
so they just break open. Roast in the oven for 20 minutes.

Mix the crushed garlic and butter to a paste, then remove the
potatoes from the oven and add the garlic butter. Toss to coat all
the potatoes then return to the oven for a further 5 minutes until
crispy and golden.

FOR THE CHERMOULA YOGURT

✦ ✦ ✦ ✦ ✦ ✦ ✦ ✦ ✦ ✦ ✦ ✦ ✦ ✦ ✦ ✦

⅔ cup (150 g) thick Greek-style
  yogurt
⅓ cup (75 g) chermoula
  (page 105)
3 tablespoons tahini

Meanwhile, mix together the ingredients for the chermoula yogurt
and set aside.

Dollop the chermoula yogurt onto a large platter, then pile the crispy,
buttery potatoes on top. Sprinkle over the parsley, scallions, sumac,
and a little more salt and pepper to taste, then serve immediately.

TO SERVE

✦ ✦ ✦ ✦ ✦ ✦ ✦ ✦ ✦ ✦ ✦ ✦ ✦ ✦ ✦ ✦

Small bunch of parsley,
  finely chopped
4 scallions, very finely sliced
1 teaspoon sumac

114   APPETIZERS, MEZZE & DIPS

FALAFEL

People ask how many falafel you should make, but in my opinion there is no such thing as too many falafel! If it's too much for you, your neighbor can have some — in Damascus, if our neighbors can smell what we're cooking, we have to take over a small plate of it for them to taste.

Falafel are not made with cooked chickpeas, but with dried chickpeas soaked in water, so you absolutely cannot use chickpeas from a can or jar. I use a traditional meat grinder to make falafel, which is a good investment if you're going to make them a lot. Otherwise, you can use a food processor, although it will make a wetter mixture. The nice thing about Damascan falafel is it doesn't include any fresh herbs, which means there's no chance of them getting soggy as they cook.

You can serve falafel on a plate, as part of a mezze. Or use them in a wrap or pita, as on page 122.

Sumac and tahini are a must for serving.

TO MAKE

✤ ✤ ✤ ✤ ✤ ✤ ✤ ✤ ✤ ✤ ✤ ✤ ✤ ✤ ✤ ✤ ✤

2 ¾ cups (500 g) dried
   chickpeas, soaked for at least
   14 hours (see instructions on
   page 68)
4 garlic cloves
½ onion, roughly chopped
   or quartered
1 teaspoon garlic powder
2 tablespoons ground coriander
1 tablespoon ground cumin
½ teaspoon baking soda
1 tablespoon salt
⅓ cup (50 g) sesame seeds
½ – ⅔ cup (115 – 150 ml) room-
   temperature water
Canola oil, for deep-frying

Put the soaked, drained chickpeas with the garlic and onion through a meat grinder into a bowl (or process in a food processor if you don't have a meat grinder). Then stir in the spices, baking soda, and salt. If you are using a food processor, pulse it gently; it should have a fine-ish sandy consistency. You can use the falafel mixture straight away or keep it in the fridge at this stage for up to 2 days.

Mix in the sesame seeds and enough water to be able to gather a ball of mixture and for it to loosely stay together. It shouldn't be too wet — just enough to form a loose patty.

Pour a 4 in (10 cm) depth of oil into a deep, heavy-based pot and heat to 350°F (180°C). To test if the oil is hot enough, drop in a little piece of falafel; if it bubbles and rises to the top, you are ready to go.

I use a special falafel tool for shaping, which you can pick up fairly inexpensively online. My falafel have a hole in the middle, resulting in a crisper texture. Otherwise, use 2 spoons to shape the mixture, or you can just roll into balls and flatten them down with your hands. Your falafel should be about 1½ in (4 cm) across.

Carefully lower the shaped falafels into the hot oil, in batches so you don't overcrowd the pot (or the temperature of the oil will drop and you won't have nice crispy falafel).

Let them crisp up for 2 minutes until golden brown, then move the oil around a little to cook them evenly all over. They should be fully cooked, golden brown, and crisp in 4 minutes. Scoop out with a slotted spoon onto paper towels to absorb excess oil.

FALAFEL WRAP

Put each of the wrap ingredients in a bowl on the table so people can make their own, adding as much or as little as they like.

TO MAKE

✤ ✤ ✤ ✤ ✤ ✤ ✤ ✤ ✤ ✤ ✤ ✤ ✤ ✤ ✤ ✤ ✤

Breads — pita bread or flatbreads (see page 82 for homemade)
Hummus (page 68)
5 or 6 falafels per person
Sliced pickled cucumbers (optional, page 56)
Sliced tomato halves
Lemon slices
Chopped parsley
Pickled chiles/Aleppo chile flakes
Tahini sauce (page 54)
Sumac

Spread each bread with a generous spoonful of hummus. Smash the falafel on top of the hummus, pressing it down into the hummus. Top with pickled cucumber slices, diced tomato, lemon slices, chopped parsley, pickled chiles or chile flakes, a drizzle of tahini sauce, and a pinch of sumac.

THE MOMENT I ARRIVED in London, I felt free. In every other city I had been in, the ten countries I'd traveled across, people would look at me and I would assume they would think, "Oh, another Syrian refugee coming through." In London, I was invisible. I looked like everyone else. There are people from all nationalities, all doing their own thing. No one even noticed me. I was in awe. I fell in love with this city immediately.

My journey from Syria to the UK is one that thousands of Syrians have taken. It's not a choice we make, we don't choose to be refugees. It's not like we decided one day to leave behind a comfortable life to live in Europe. And the journey is every bit as difficult, as exhausting, as dehumanizing, as frightening as you imagine it is from the stories you've already heard.

My story, like so many others, began with me leaving my family behind in Damascus. I knew it was unsafe for them there; in another life before all this, I couldn't have imagined leaving them in this way, but it was our only option. I fear for the future of Syria and can't even bring myself to imagine our life if we were all still there today. Getting to safety, and then getting them to join me, was the only way out.

From Damascus, I traveled by car into Lebanon and then on up through Turkey. In Turkey I was put in touch with a smuggler who I paid so I could get on a boat to Greece. It was a small, rubber dingy designed to hold nine people. There were 56 of us crammed in, including a pregnant woman and 12 children. I have no idea how it didn't sink, how we all survived. Thinking about it now, about the risks we were all taking, still haunts me. But arriving in Greece — in Europe! — was the most incredible feeling. It was August 2, 2015. I won't ever forget. By this stage in all of our journeys, though, having come so far already, having left so much behind, with so much uncertainty still ahead, we were broken people. Whoever we used to be when we lived in Syria was gone, we were brought down to nothing, we had been made to feel like we were nothing. But, for a little while in Greece we had our humanity restored. We were met by volunteers who welcomed us, who showed us the way to go next, who made us feel safe. The Greek coast guards had rescue boats that they'd launch into the sea, but instead of helping those refugees who were making that terrifying journey across the water, they'd damage their boats, they'd prevent them landing on the shores. I have learned so many lessons about myself, about human beings, about the world since the war started, but the most powerful realization I have come to is that there are two types of people. Yes, there are those who willingly sabotage the boats of desperate people fleeing for their lives. But there are also those who will welcome you with open arms, with love, with handwritten signs that read "You are safe." I had left Syria with my faith in everything completely destroyed, but my journey, however dangerous at times, has helped me believe in the goodness in people again.

From Greece, I walked hundreds of miles to Macedonia, and then caught a train into Serbia. I biked all the way through Serbia, and another smuggler helped me into Hungary. The boat crossing to Greece was traumatizing, but I think the most difficult part of the journey for me was in Hungary. Six men, including me, hiding in the back of an old Peugeot with the back seats taken out. Can you imagine trying to fit us all in? And then out of nowhere a seventh man jumped in to join us. We had no choice but to let him come with us, since he'd have shouted and given us away if we'd said no. We were crammed in, squashed up against each other for four hours as our driver, who was drunk, drove us to Vienna. When we arrived, he shouted for us to get out, but all of our arms and legs were totally numb and none of us could move.

From Vienna, another train took me to Stuttgart, in Germany, and for many refugees, this is where their journey ends. Germany has helped so many people find refuge, to begin new lives, and I could have stayed there too. But I had family in England, I spoke English already. I was too old to learn a new language and I needed to speak it well so I could work. So I carried on from Germany to Paris. I spent a couple of nights in Paris, while I rested and figured out what to do next. That was when I started to hear the word Calais. I'd heard of Calais before, in passing, in my former life as a textiler back in Syria and in Dubai. There is a beautiful, silk-like fabric called Dantelle de Calais — Made in Calais — that is used for making wedding dresses. It felt like a sign: I was going to Calais.

When I arrived in Calais, it was not as I'd imagined. It was terrifying. The Jungle — the camp where refugees like me were staying — was too dangerous, too crowded. In the area around it, the air was charged with a strange energy, like something bad could happen at any minute. Instead, I slept on the steps of a church for 64 days with several other Syrian refugees. I'd left Syria nine days before, and then here I was for two months, with many, many failed attempts to cross into the UK. The church was empty, mostly unused except for funerals, when we would remove our belongings and clean the entrance way. You'd think I would have been at my lowest at this point and yet here was where my hope returned. I found cooking again, with one knife (no more, in case people thought I was a threat) and a small hot plate donated to us. We'd get leftovers from the supermarket, from the Carrefour, and with those leftovers, with whatever we had, I'd cook the dishes I loved from home, adapted, of course, depending on what we had, and people found joy where they could in eating what I made. I think it restored in all of us the faith that things could, and would, get better.

The closest I came to successfully making it across to the UK was on a trip back to Paris. I'd been put in touch with a smuggler there, who connected me with another Syrian, Hassan Akkad. I didn't know him, but we'd been neighbors in Damascus and we knew each other's friends. He had been filming parts of his journey on his phone and his story was later used in the BAFTA-winning documentary series, *Exodus: Our Journey to Europe*. He's a great friend of mine now, but back then I just thought he was one of the smugglers, and neither of us quite trusted each other. Hassan delivered a fake ID to me, and brought it to where I was staying in Paris. When he arrived at the hotel, I was wearing the same shirt as in the photo and he told me to change as it'd be too obvious it wasn't genuine. The plan was for us to fly from Charles de Gaulle airport into Heathrow. Hassan would go after me and, if I was successful, he'd follow on the next flight. If I didn't make it, I'd go back to Paris and I'd get my money back. It was all incredibly organized — honestly, the smuggler network is more efficient than the UK Home Office!

Hours later, I was standing at the airport gate waiting to board an EasyJet flight to the UK, my fake Greek passport in my hand, my new name, Buros. It was all going to be OK. This was it, the moment I'd been dreaming of for months. Then, I heard a voice over the loudspeakers calling for Buros. I froze. I was told I had to go to the ticket office as there was a problem with my ticket.

Entering the ticket office, I had no idea what was about to happen. But I knew it couldn't be good. The woman behind the desk asked me where my passport had come from and I told her it was mine. She then handed me a piece of paper with some Greek written on it. I looked down at it and my heart sank. She said, "if you can read this, I'll let you go." It was all over. I told her I couldn't read it, but that I was just doing my best. I was just trying to do what I could for my family. To be safe. She looked right at me and told me that the police would be in her office in five minutes. I sank down, defeated. But then, she said "no, no, you don't understand. You have five minutes before the police get here — go!". I couldn't believe what I was hearing. I had five minutes to escape. She told me to get on the train, not to wait for the bus, and to head back to Paris. I made it outside into the fresh air and still couldn't take in what had just happened. I didn't have enough money for the train, so I stood at the bus stop waiting. Then I saw the woman again, she'd followed me out and asked me why I was still there. When I explained, she gave me her own metro ticket and also her phone number. Before she left she took my arm and told me that my ID was great, it was a really great passport, but whoever had arranged my flight had already booked fifty people one-way on the same credit card and that's why it had been flagged. She said goodbye and, as so often on this crazy journey, I felt as though I'd been saved by an angel.

Hassan was in jail. He'd never made it across to the UK. He didn't even board his flight. The police left him in a bare cell overnight and then drove him up the highway and left him on the side of the road in the pouring rain. We didn't have each other's phone numbers, but he came to the hotel where he'd delivered my passport, to the hotel I was staying in, hoping I'd be there. My room phone rang, and reception said I had a visitor downstairs. I didn't know what to expect because I didn't know anyone! When Hassan saw me, he started crying. He was cold, wet, miserable, and completely lost. They'd told him I was in the UK, and so seeing each other was an incredibly emotional moment for us both. We were reunited, afraid, still stuck in Paris, but alive and free. We had to make a new plan. In the morning we headed back to Calais.

DUKKAH SALAD

SERVES 2 AS A MAIN
OR 4 AS A SIDE

Heirloom tomatoes, roasted fennel, and dukkah

Make this in summer when the tomatoes are at their best. The better the tomato, the better this will taste, so splash out and get the good ones.

TO MAKE

❖ ❖ ❖ ❖ ❖ ❖ ❖ ❖ ❖ ❖ ❖ ❖ ❖ ❖ ❖ ❖ ❖

1 fennel bulb

2 tablespoons olive oil

1 teaspoon za'atar

10½ oz (300 g) assorted heirloom tomatoes, cut into chunks

2 tablespoons good-quality extra virgin olive oil

Grated zest and juice of ½ lemon

2 tablespoons dukkah (page 29)

5½ oz (150 g) soft goat cheese

Small handful of fresh tarragon leaves

Salt

Preheat the oven to 400°F (200°C).

Cut the fennel bulb into 6 – 8 wedges, depending on how large it is. Toss in the olive oil, za'atar, and salt to taste, place on a baking sheet, and roast for 25 – 30 minutes until soft, slightly crisp, and golden. Set aside to cool slightly.

Toss the tomatoes in a little salt and the extra virgin olive oil, lemon zest and juice, and dukkah. Roughly crumble the cheese and place on a large serving plate, followed by the roasted fennel and then the tomatoes. Finish with the tarragon leaves.

HARAA ASBAEU

Sometimes when I can't find the right pasta for this, I buy pappardelle or fettuccine and either chop it up if it's fresh, or scrunch up dried to make small pieces.

FOR THE TAMARIND SAUCE

❖ ❖ ❖ ❖ ❖ ❖ ❖ ❖ ❖ ❖ ❖ ❖ ❖ ❖ ❖ ❖

1¼ oz (35 g) block of dried tamarind
Scant 1 cup (200 ml) water

To make the tamarind sauce, crumble the dried tamarind block into a saucepan and add the water. Bring to a boil over medium heat and boil for at least 30 minutes to extract all the flavor and reduce the water. Strain through a sieve into a bowl; use a spoon to squash it through and scrape underneath into the bowl. You'll be left with a little under a ½ cup (100 ml) and will have a really intense flavor. If you end up with a bit less than this, that's fine — it's all about the flavor.

TO MAKE

❖ ❖ ❖ ❖ ❖ ❖ ❖ ❖ ❖ ❖ ❖ ❖ ❖ ❖ ❖ ❖

2 flatbreads (see page 82 for homemade) or flour tortillas
1 tablespoon olive oil
1 teaspoon sumac
1¼ cups (250 g) dried brown lentils
6⅓ cups (1.5 liters) just-boiled water
7 oz (200 g) small square pasta (or any small pasta, or see introduction)
5 tablespoons cilantro oil (page 37)
2 tablespoons pomegranate molasses
1 teaspoon ground cumin
1 quantity crispy onions (page 54)
Handful of pomegranate seeds
Salt

Preheat the oven to 400°F (200°C).

Cut the flatbreads into ½ in (1 cm) strips and toss with the olive oil, sumac, and a pinch of salt. Spread out on a baking sheet and place in the oven for 3–5 minutes until crisp and toasted.

Wash the lentils, then place in a pot with the just-boiled water. Add salt and boil for 20 minutes until just cooked. Now stir in the pasta and boil for 5–8 minutes, depending on the type and size, until cooked. You should still have a tiny bit of water left in the pot; if not, add a little more boiling water as you want a silky, wet mixture. Take off the heat.

While the lentils and pasta are still warm, add the cilantro oil, making sure you're getting a good amount of the chopped cilantro leaves too. Stir in the tamarind sauce, a little more salt if needed, the pomegranate molasses, and ground cumin. Tip the lentil and pasta mixture onto a large platter and allow to cool completely.

Traditionally we plate the toppings in stripes, starting with the cilantro leaves from the oil, then crispy onions, crispy flatbreads, followed by pomegranate seeds, then repeat.

SAJ

TO MAKE

✤ ✤ ✤ ✤ ✤ ✤ ✤ ✤ ✤ ✤ ✤ ✤ ✤ ✤ ✤ ✤

1 quantity of flatbread dough
  (page 82)

Make the dough according to the instructions on page 82 and leave
to rise.

When your dough has risen, whisk the egg in a bowl, then stir
in the halloumi, parsley, and chile flakes. Or, if using the za'atar, mix
together the oil and za'atar in a small bowl. Knock back the dough,
divide into 12 equal pieces, and roll each into a ball. Set aside to rest
for 15 – 20 minutes, then roll each ball into a 6 in (15 cm) circle, by
only pushing the rolling pin away from you, turning the dough after
each roll (not back and forth; this is to help get an even flatbread).
At this point I lift the flatbread onto a mukhada — a pillowy surface
to help stretch the dough — but you can skip this if you don't have one.

FOR THE TOPPING

✤ ✤ ✤ ✤ ✤ ✤ ✤ ✤ ✤ ✤ ✤ ✤ ✤ ✤ ✤ ✤

1 egg
3½ oz (100 g) halloumi, grated
Small handful of parsley,
  finely chopped
Pinch of chile flakes
OR
3 tablespoons good-quality olive oil
2 tablespoons za'atar

Place a nonstick frying pan over medium-high heat and flip
a flatbread into the pan. Cook for 30 – 40 seconds until lightly
brown, then flip over and spoon on your topping of choice
(the cheese and egg mix or the za'atar oil). Turn down the heat
to medium and continue to cook for 1 – 2 minutes until the cheese
has melted (if using) and the flatbread is crisp on the bottom.

Serve straight away, while hot.

BATATA HARRA

SERVES 4 AS A SIDE

TO MAKE

✧ ✧ ✧ ✧ ✧ ✧ ✧ ✧ ✧ ✧ ✧ ✧ ✧ ✧ ✧ ✧ ✧

4 – 5 medium-sized Idaho
  or Yukon Gold potatoes,
  peeled and cut into 1¼ in
  (3 cm) cubes
¼ cup (60 ml) olive oil
5 confit garlic cloves (page 53)
  or 2 peeled raw garlic cloves
½ teaspoon chile flakes
½ teaspoon ground cumin
½ teaspoon smoked paprika
Large handful of cilantro leaves,
  chopped
2 tablespoons extra virgin olive oil
Salt and ground black pepper

Preheat the oven to 425°F (220°C).

Put the potatoes in a large, low-sided roasting pan, toss through the
¼ cup (60 ml) of olive oil and a good pinch each of salt and pepper.

Roast in the oven for 30 minutes until crisp and golden all over.

In a small bowl, crush the garlic cloves, then mix in the chile flakes,
cumin, smoked paprika, and chopped cilantro, along with the extra
virgin olive oil. Remove the potatoes from the oven, toss in the spice
mix, and serve immediately.

134   APPETIZERS, MEZZE & DIPS

FOUR

MAINS

SHURABAT ADAS

Lentil soup

TO MAKE

❖ ❖ ❖ ❖ ❖ ❖ ❖ ❖ ❖ ❖ ❖ ❖ ❖ ❖ ❖ ❖ ❖ ❖ ❖

1 cup (200 g) red lentils
¼ cup (50 g) short-grain rice
⅓ cup (50 g) freekeh
2 tablespoons olive oil
1 tablespoon cumin seeds
2 onions, finely chopped
2 small carrots, peeled and
   roughly chopped
2 garlic cloves, finely chopped
1 teaspoon ground cumin
2 tablespoons safflower,
   plus extra to garnish
1 teaspoon ground black pepper
½ teaspoon ground coriander
2 tablespoons tomato paste
7 cups (1.7 liters) vegetable or
   chicken stock or water
Salt

Start by washing the lentils, rice, and freekeh together in a large
sieve until the water runs clear.

In a tall, large pot, heat the olive oil over medium heat, then add the
cumin seeds and toast for a minute. Now add the onions and carrots
and cook for 5–8 minutes until soft and a little caramelized. Add the
garlic and cook for a further 1–2 minutes until softened.

Add the lentils, rice, and freekeh and stir to toast all the grains for
2 minutes before mixing in the ground cumin, 1 tablespoon of the
safflower, the black pepper, ground coriander, tomato paste, and
2 teaspoons of salt. Once everything is nicely toasted and coated in
spices, add the stock or water so it covers everything by at least
2½ in (6 cm).

Bring to a boil, then turn down the heat and simmer for 1 hour until
everything is soft.

Process to a thick soup in a blender, adding more water if you prefer
a thinner consistency, then add the remaining safflower. Taste and
season as necessary.

TO SERVE

❖ ❖ ❖ ❖ ❖ ❖ ❖ ❖ ❖ ❖ ❖ ❖ ❖ ❖ ❖ ❖ ❖ ❖ ❖

Light cream (or mozzarella,
   torn into small pieces)
Small handful of chives,
   finely chopped
4 pita breads, toasted

Ladle into bowls and top with cream or mozzarella, chives,
and a sprinkle of safflower, and serve with toasted pita bread.

KITIF GHANAM

Lamb shoulder

FOR THE MARINADE

❖ ❖ ❖ ❖ ❖ ❖ ❖ ❖ ❖ ❖ ❖ ❖ ❖ ❖ ❖ ❖ ❖

5 garlic cloves, grated
2 tablespoons smoked paprika
1 tablespoon mild Madras
   curry powder
½ tablespoon ground black pepper
1¼ in (3 cm) piece of fresh
   ginger, grated
1 tablespoon baharat (page 32)
Juice of 1 lemon
1 tablespoon tomato paste
2 tablespoons red pepper paste
Good pinch of salt
⅔ cup (150 ml) olive oil

Mix together all the marinade ingredients in a large container.

Rub the marinade all over the lamb so it's completely covered. Cover and marinate in the fridge for a minimum of 4 hours, ideally overnight.

TO MAKE

❖ ❖ ❖ ❖ ❖ ❖ ❖ ❖ ❖ ❖ ❖ ❖ ❖ ❖ ❖ ❖ ❖

3 lb 5 oz – 4½ lb (1.5 – 2 kg)
   lamb shoulder, bone in
10 garlic cloves, peeled
4 sprigs of thyme
4 sprigs of rosemary
handful of chopped onions,
   carrots, and/or potatoes
   (optional)

When you're ready to cook, preheat the oven to 320°F (160°C).

Take the lamb from the fridge, then get a high-sided roasting pan and line with a layer of foil and a layer of parchment paper, large enough to cover the lamb. Add the garlic and herb sprigs to the middle, followed by the lamb and all the marinade (you can also add the onions, carrots, or potatoes at this stage, if you like). Fold the foil and parchment paper over the lamb like a parcel, then flip it over and wrap it again in another layer of foil so the lamb is tightly wrapped and there are no gaps. We want to cook the lamb in its own juices, so it's really important that it's completely covered at this stage.

Place in the oven and cook for 4 hours or until the meat is falling off the bone. Remove from the oven, unwrap, increase the temperature to 400°F (200°C), and roast until browned on top.

TO SERVE

❖ ❖ ❖ ❖ ❖ ❖ ❖ ❖ ❖ ❖ ❖ ❖ ❖ ❖ ❖ ❖

Kabsa rice (page 166) or
   plain bulgur (page 49)

Serve with all its juices. This is best with kabsa rice or plain bulgur.

KEBAB HINDI

Ground lamb koftas in rich tomato sauce

Hindi means "from India," but this dish isn't from India, it's a Damascene recipe — and the funny thing about it is that in India they have a Chammi kebab (meaning from Damascus, because in the old days it was called Chamma), but it has nothing to do with Damascus! Even with food people are always crossing over and sharing, but in this case the name comes from Indian family coming to settle in Syria a long time ago. This is a classic recipe that I had nothing to do with creating.

Even at home we don't waste food. We eat it the next day, so we don't worry if we make a lot of this. I prefer the chile paste hot, but feel free to change it — my wife doesn't really like it hot. If you don't have the chile paste or don't want to use it, tomato paste is fine — just use an extra ½ tablespoon. Serve with a green plate (page 45).

Pictured overleaf.

FOR THE TOMATO SAUCE

✧ ✧ ✧ ✧ ✧ ✧ ✧ ✧ ✧ ✧ ✧ ✧ ✧ ✧ ✧ ✧ ✧ ✧ ✧ ✧

2 tablespoons olive oil
1 teaspoon cumin seeds
2 medium onions, diced
2 x 14 oz (400 g) cans of
  chopped tomatoes
1 tablespoon tomato paste
1 tablespoon chile paste
  (see introduction)

Heat the olive oil for the tomato sauce in a saucepan over medium heat and add the cumin seeds. Cook, stirring, for 30–60 seconds, until the seeds start to pop and toast. Add the onions and cook for 5–7 minutes until they soften and caramelize a little, then add the tomatoes. When it starts to simmer, add the tomato paste and chile paste. Stirring often, cook for 25–40 minutes over medium heat, with the lid on. You will know it's cooked by tasting: it will taste of cooked tomatoes. Take off the heat and let it cool down to room temperature or a little warmer. Pour it into a 12 in (30 cm) roasting pan or dish to help it cool down — we are going to use the roasting pan for the koftas.

Preheat the oven to 400°F (200°C).

FOR THE KOFTAS

✧ ✧ ✧ ✧ ✧ ✧ ✧ ✧ ✧ ✧ ✧ ✧ ✧ ✧ ✧ ✧ ✧ ✧ ✧ ✧

1 medium onion, roughly chopped
2 garlic cloves, peeled
1 teaspoon baharat (page 32)
½ teaspoon sea salt flakes
½ teaspoon coarsely ground
  black pepper
1 lb 2 oz (500 g) ground lamb
Olive oil, for drizzling

In a food processor, blend the onion, garlic, baharat, salt, and black pepper to make a paste. Then add the lamb and pulse to combine. Shape the mixture into 20 balls. Squeeze each ball in your hands to make a small kebab shape in your fist. Place on top of the tomato sauce in the roasting pan. Don't worry that the sauce is still quite watery — that's OK. Arrange them close to each other because they will shrink down as they cook in the oven.

Drizzle with a little olive oil and bake in the oven for 30 minutes, to reduce the sauce and cook the kebabs through.

TO SERVE

✧ ✧ ✧ ✧ ✧ ✧ ✧ ✧ ✧ ✧ ✧ ✧ ✧ ✧ ✧ ✧ ✧ ✧ ✧ ✧

Chopped parsley (as much
  as you like, but at least
  ½ handful)
½ handful of toasted pine nuts

To serve, top with chopped parsley and toasted pine nuts.

ZAHRA HARRA

Cauliflower, red onions, and red peppers

FOR THE MARINADE

✧ ✧ ✧ ✧ ✧ ✧ ✧ ✧ ✧ ✧ ✧ ✧ ✧ ✧ ✧ ✧ ✧ ✧ ✧

5 garlic cloves, minced
2 tablespoons tomato paste
1 tablespoon harissa paste
Scant ½ cup (100 ml) olive oil

Mix the marinade ingredients together in a small bowl, with a pinch each of salt and black pepper.

If your cauliflower has a lot of leaves, remove the toughest leaves from the outside, leaving the lighter ones attached. Chop the cauliflower into 8 wedges then coat them in three-quarters of the marinade so that all the gaps are coated. At this stage you can marinate them for up to 12 hours, but you can also cook them straight away.

TO MAKE

✧ ✧ ✧ ✧ ✧ ✧ ✧ ✧ ✧ ✧ ✧ ✧ ✧ ✧ ✧ ✧ ✧ ✧ ✧

1 large cauliflower
1 red onion
2 red Romano peppers
1 teaspoon dried or fresh thyme
1 teaspoon sumac

Preheat the oven to 400°F (200°C) and line a large low-sided baking sheet with parchment paper. Add the cauliflower wedges to the lined pan and roast for 15 minutes.

While the cauliflower is roasting, chop the red onion and red peppers into similar-sized pieces (about 1¼ in/3 cm) and, in a bowl, coat with the remaining marinade and the thyme and sumac. Remove the cauliflower from the oven and turn each wedge over. Add the onions and peppers to the pan and put back in the oven for a further 25 minutes until the cauliflower is crispy and golden and the onions and peppers are soft.

TO SERVE

✧ ✧ ✧ ✧ ✧ ✧ ✧ ✧ ✧ ✧ ✧ ✧ ✧ ✧ ✧ ✧ ✧ ✧ ✧

Tahini sauce (page 54)
Cilantro oil (page 37)
Aleppo chile flakes
Salt and ground black pepper

Serve immediately with a little more salt and pepper and the tahini sauce, cilantro oil, and chile flakes.

FASULIA BIL ZAYT

Green beans and tomato sauce

This is a great side dish or a vegan/vegetarian main. You can make it in advance, since it's served at room temperature.

TO MAKE

✧ ✧ ✧ ✧ ✧ ✧ ✧ ✧ ✧ ✧ ✧ ✧ ✧ ✧ ✧ ✧ ✧

1 lb (450 g) fine green beans, tails trimmed
2 tablespoons olive oil
1 teaspoon cumin seeds
5 garlic cloves, very thinly sliced
1–2 red chiles, very thinly sliced (optional)
1 tablespoon tomato paste
1 tablespoon red pepper paste
1 x 14 oz (400 g) can of chopped tomatoes
1 teaspoon ground cumin
1 teaspoon ground black pepper
Good pinch of salt

Boil the beans in a large pot of salted water for 3–4 minutes, until just cooked. Drain and set aside.

In the same pot, over medium heat, add the olive oil and cumin seeds and toast for a minute before adding the garlic and chiles and frying for a minute. Add the tomato paste and pepper paste, stir to cook out for a few minutes, then add the chopped tomatoes. Stir in the ground cumin, pepper, and salt, then simmer for 10–15 minutes until you have a thick, rich sauce.

Add the green beans for the last few minutes then turn off the heat and allow to cool to room temperature.

TO SERVE

✧ ✧ ✧ ✧ ✧ ✧ ✧ ✧ ✧ ✧ ✧ ✧ ✧ ✧ ✧

Tahini sauce (page 54)
Green plate (page 45)
Greek-style yogurt (optional)

Serve with tahini sauce, a green plate, and a dollop of yogurt on the side, if you like.

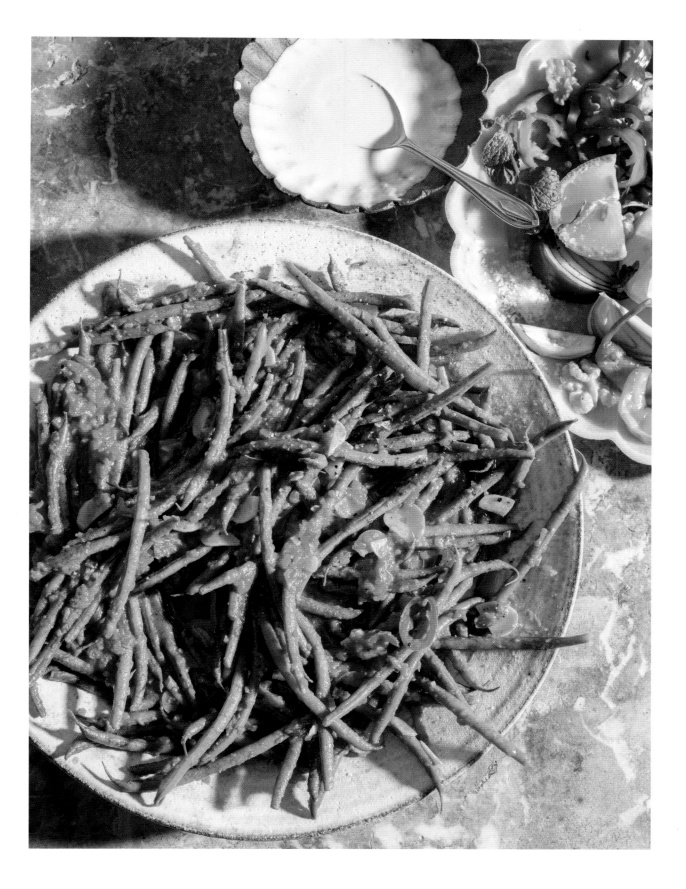

MAHASHI

Stuffed vine leaves

If you can't find high-fat ground lamb, add 1 tablespoon of ghee.

FOR THE VINE LEAF STUFFING

✤ ✤ ✤ ✤ ✤ ✤ ✤ ✤ ✤ ✤ ✤ ✤ ✤ ✤ ✤ ✤ ✤ ✤ ✤

1 cup (200 g) short-grain
  Egyptian rice
2 tablespoons safflower
2 teaspoons ground cumin
1 teaspoon ground black pepper
1 teaspoon baharat (page 32)
14 oz (400 g) high-fat (30%)
  ground lamb
50 vine leaves (see introduction
  on page 76)
Salt

Wash the rice until the water runs clear then drain, put in a bowl with
the safflower, and mix thoroughly (wearing gloves to save your hands
from turning yellow!). Add the cumin, black pepper, baharat, ground
lamb, and a good pinch of salt, then mix again with your hands.

Prepare your vine leaves (see introduction on page 76) then lay one
out, ideally on a tray, in front of you. Spoon 1 tablespoon of the rice
and lamb mixture into the middle of the leaf. Fold the sides inwards
like an envelope, then roll away from you, making a neat little roll.
Set aside on another tray and continue with the rest until you have
used all the leaves and filling.

FOR THE SAUCE

✤ ✤ ✤ ✤ ✤ ✤ ✤ ✤ ✤ ✤ ✤ ✤ ✤ ✤ ✤ ✤ ✤

Juice of 4 lemons
2 cups (500 ml) water
1 whole garlic head, cloves peeled
  and smashed to a paste
1 teaspoon ground black pepper
1 teaspoon baharat (page 32)
2 teaspoons salt
1 tablespoon tomato paste

Put the lemon juice and water in another bowl, then add the garlic,
black pepper, baharat, salt, and the tomato paste and mix together
until combined.

TO MAKE

✦ ✦ ✦ ✦ ✦ ✦ ✦ ✦ ✦ ✦ ✦ ✦ ✦ ✦ ✦ ✦ ✦ ✦ ✦

2 starchy potatoes, peeled and
    cut into ½ in (1 cm) slices
1 lb 12 oz (800 g) lamb neck,
    sliced into ¾ in (2 cm) pieces
    (ask your butcher to do this)
2 whole garlic heads
1 jar of artichoke hearts, drained
    (optional)
Plain yogurt, to serve

In a wide, heavy-based pot or Dutch oven, about 12 in (30 cm) in
diameter, layer the sliced potatoes to completely cover the base.
Now add the lamb neck in one layer, placing the slices so they fit
tightly together. Add the stuffed vine leaves on top of the lamb neck,
laying them tightly around the edge of the dish in concentric rings
and stacking them on top of each other, until the final 2 layers, where
you want to leave a gap in the middle.

Place the garlic heads in the gap in the middle, along with the
artichokes, if using, then place a weight on top of everything.
I have a traditional weight that is meant for this dish, but if you
don't, then stack 3–5 plates on top instead, which works fine.

Pour in the sauce to just cover everything; you might not need all of
it, so set aside the rest in case you need to top it up later. Tightly cover
the pot with foil or a lid then place over high heat until the liquid
is boiling. Boil for 10 minutes, then turn the heat down to low and
simmer for 1 hour.

Remove the lid, put a little pressure on the weight or plates, tilt
the pot, and carefully drain as much of the liquid as you can into a
bowl. Remove the weight and the garlic heads and artichokes (if
using), then place a serving platter or tray on top of the pot. Very
quickly and carefully flip the pot over so it's upside down on the tray.

Gently lift the pot up, revealing the layers of the potato, meat,
and vine leaves.

Place the garlic and artichokes back on top of the potatoes
and serve with the sauce you saved earlier, and some yogurt.

JAJ BIL FURN

Grilled chicken thighs

This is a staple, midweek, one-pan meal. You can use any vegetables, too, so it's a great way to use up anything you have in the fridge.

FOR THE MARINADE

❖ ❖ ❖ ❖ ❖ ❖ ❖ ❖ ❖ ❖ ❖ ❖ ❖ ❖ ❖ ❖ ❖

1 teaspoon tomato paste
2 tablespoons shish taouk
  (page 33)
1 teaspoon mild Madras
  curry powder
5 garlic cloves, crushed
1 tablespoon ground black pepper
2 tablespoons Greek-style yogurt
Good pinch of salt
2 tablespoons white wine vinegar
Scant ½ cup (100 ml) olive oil

In a bowl, mix together all the marinade ingredients, adding the oil last. Take out 2 tablespoons and set aside for later.

TO MAKE

❖ ❖ ❖ ❖ ❖ ❖ ❖ ❖ ❖ ❖ ❖ ❖ ❖ ❖ ❖ ❖ ❖

8 chicken thighs, skin on and
  bone in
2 carrots, chopped into
  2 in (5 cm) chunks
2 large floury potatoes,
  chopped into 2 in (5 cm)
  chunks
1 onion, peeled and cut into
  6 wedges
5½ oz (150 g) baby chestnut
  mushrooms

Add the chicken to the marinade and mix well so the pieces are all evenly coated. Cover and marinate in the fridge for a minimum of 2 hours, ideally overnight.

When you're ready to cook, preheat the oven to 400°F (200°C) and remove the chicken from the fridge.

Put all the vegetables in a large roasting pan. Place the chicken thighs on top, skin side up, wrap the tray tightly in foil, and cook for 25 minutes, then remove from the oven, remove the foil, and brush the chicken with the reserved marinade. Return to the oven for a further 20 minutes until the chicken skin is crispy. You may need to turn up your oven here to get a crispy skin.

TO SERVE

❖ ❖ ❖ ❖ ❖ ❖ ❖ ❖ ❖ ❖ ❖ ❖ ❖ ❖ ❖ ❖ ❖

Cooked rice and/or
  tabbouleh (page 100)

Serve immediately with rice or tabbouleh.

SYRIAN FISH AND CHIPS WITH TAHINI SAUCE

FOR THE FISH

✦ ✦ ✦ ✦ ✦ ✦ ✦ ✦ ✦ ✦ ✦ ✦ ✦ ✦ ✦ ✦ ✦ ✦ ✦

4 fillets of haddock
2 teaspoons ground cumin
1 teaspoon ground white pepper
4 garlic cloves, crushed
3½ tablespoons olive oil
1⅔ cups (200 g) all-purpose flour
1 tablespoon cornstarch

Put the haddock in a dish. In a bowl, mix the cumin, white pepper, garlic, olive oil, and a pinch of salt. Pour this over the fish, cover, and leave to marinate in the fridge for at least 4 hours, or overnight.

FOR THE TAHINI SAUCE

✦ ✦ ✦ ✦ ✦ ✦ ✦ ✦ ✦ ✦ ✦ ✦ ✦ ✦ ✦ ✦ ✦ ✦

3 tablespoons tahini
1 garlic clove, crushed
Juice of 1 lemon
Small handful of parsley, chopped
1 tablespoon ice-cold water

Meanwhile, make the tahini sauce. In a bowl, mix together the tahini, garlic, lemon juice, and chopped parsley. Stir in the ice-cold water until you have a creamy sauce, then set aside.

FOR THE CHIPS (FRIES)

✦ ✦ ✦ ✦ ✦ ✦ ✦ ✦ ✦ ✦ ✦ ✦ ✦ ✦ ✦ ✦ ✦ ✦

1 lb 12 oz (800 g) potatoes, ideally Idaho or Yukon Gold
8½ cups (2 liters) sunflower or vegetable oil
1 teaspoon smoked paprika
Salt

For the chips, peel and cut the potatoes into finger-thick fries (about ½ in/1 cm). Pour the oil into a large, heavy-based pot; it should be at least 3½ in (9 cm) deep, but not over halfway up your pot. Place over medium-high heat until it reaches 285°F/140°C (if you don't have a thermometer, add a small piece of potato to the oil and if it floats to the top and fries, you're good to go). Add the potato pieces in small batches and fry for around 8 minutes until very lightly golden and mostly cooked, transferring with a slotted spoon to paper towels.

Turn up the heat slightly (if you have a thermometer, you want it to be at 350°F/180°C, or you can test with a piece of potato again; it should turn golden much faster than the first time). Add your potatoes in batches again, and fry for 2–3 minutes until golden, transferring to new paper towels. Season generously with the paprika and salt.

Return to the fish: put the flour, a pinch of salt, and the cornstarch in a bowl and mix. Dip the fish pieces in the flour one by one until completely covered with flour. Make sure the oil is still at 350°F (180°C), then fry the fish pieces for 5–6 minutes until they turn golden and crispy. Serve with the chips and the tahini sauce.

MUJADARA

Bulgur with brown lentils

This is nice either hot or cold, so it's great to make extra and eat the next day as a salad. Use the best extra virgin olive oil you have, as your whole dish will taste of it.

TO MAKE

❖ ❖ ❖ ❖ ❖ ❖ ❖ ❖ ❖ ❖ ❖ ❖ ❖ ❖ ❖ ❖ ❖

1 cup (200 g) dried brown lentils
Scant ½ cup (100 ml) extra
    virgin olive oil
1 tablespoon cumin seeds
1 large onion, finely chopped
1 teaspoon ground black pepper
1 teaspoon baharat (page 32)
1 teaspoon mild Madras
    curry powder
1⅓ cups (200 g) coarse bulgur
Salt

Wash the lentils in a sieve until the water runs clear.

Put ⅓ cup (75 ml) of the olive oil in a medium pot with the cumin seeds over medium-high heat and toast for a minute, then turn down the heat a little, add the onion, and cook for 8–10 minutes until soft and slightly caramelized.

Tip in the lentils with 1 teaspoon of salt, then add the spices and stir to toast and coat the lentils with the oil. Add water to come about 1¼ in (3 cm) above the lentils, then cover with a lid and bring to a boil. Lower to a bubbling simmer for 20 minutes until almost cooked; you want the lentils to still be a little firm.

Now stir in the bulgur plus the remaining olive oil. Top up with boiling water if necessary so it is still 1¼ in (3 cm) above the lentils and bulgur. Cover and turn up the heat to boil for 3–5 minutes, then take off the heat. Cover the whole pot with a clean tea towel, then the lid, and set aside for 30–45 minutes.

TO SERVE

❖ ❖ ❖ ❖ ❖ ❖ ❖ ❖ ❖ ❖ ❖ ❖ ❖ ❖ ❖ ❖

Crispy onions (page 54)
Green plate (page 45)
Pickled cucumbers (page 56)
Turkish pickled peppers
Laban bi khiar (page 97)
Lemon wedges

Remove the tea towel and lid then break up the grains with a fork and taste for seasoning. Serve topped with crispy onions and your favorite sides.

MUJADARA SALAD

TO MAKE

❖ ❖ ❖ ❖ ❖ ❖ ❖ ❖ ❖ ❖ ❖ ❖ ❖ ❖ ❖ ❖ ❖

1½ – 2 cups (300 g) leftover
  mujadara (page 158)
3 baby cucumbers, finely diced
6 radishes, finely sliced
Handful of parsley,
  roughly chopped
Small handful of mint leaves,
  roughly chopped
⅓ cup (50 g) pine nuts, toasted
1 large tomato, deseeded
  and finely chopped
Juice of 1 lemon
3½ tablespoons extra virgin
  olive oil
Sea salt flakes and ground
  black pepper

Place everything in a large serving bowl, with salt and pepper to
taste, and toss together to combine.

KABSA RICE
WITH SHRIMP

TO MAKE

✦ ✦

2 tablespoons olive oil

1 tablespoon cumin seeds

3 cloves

1 cinnamon stick

3 green cardamom pods

1½ tablespoons kabsa spice
   mix (page 32)

1 teaspoon ground black pepper

1½ teaspoons baharat (page 32)

1 bay leaf

1 large onion, finely chopped

1 green pepper, deseeded and
   finely chopped

1 or 2 small red chiles (optional)

1 x 14 oz (400 g) can of tomatoes

2 teaspoons salt

2 cups (400 g) American golden
   rice (or other long-grain rice)

½ cup (75 g) raisins or golden
   raisins

10½ oz (300 g) peeled raw
   jumbo shrimp

Heat the olive oil in a large, heavy-based pot over medium-high heat then add the cumin seeds and toast for a minute. Add all the remaining spices and the bay leaf and cook for a further minute, stirring continuously. Add the onion and green pepper and fry for 10 minutes until soft, stirring regularly and turning the heat down if needed to ensure the spices don't catch. If you want to add a chile or two, slice in half lengthways and add to the pot.

Add the tomatoes and salt, then fill the empty tomato can with water and pour it in. Bring everything to a boil then turn down to a simmer for 25 minutes.

Meanwhile, wash the rice in a sieve until the water runs clear, then place in a bowl with enough water to cover. Soak for 30 minutes.

Taste the sauce at this point, making sure the seasoning is right, then drain the rice and stir it into the pot, along with the raisins and shrimp, making sure you have about ¾ in (2 cm) of liquid above the rice; if not, add a little more water.

Bring the rice back up to a boil, then put the lid on and immediately turn it right down to the lowest simmer for 15 minutes. Take off the heat, leaving the lid tightly on, and rest for 10 minutes.

TO SERVE

✦ ✦

⅓ cup (50 g) pine nuts, toasted

Handful of chopped parsley

Laban bi khiar (page 97)

Green salad

Lift the lid on the rice and stir it gently with a fork to break up the grains, then serve with the pine nuts, parsley, laban bi khiar, and a green salad.

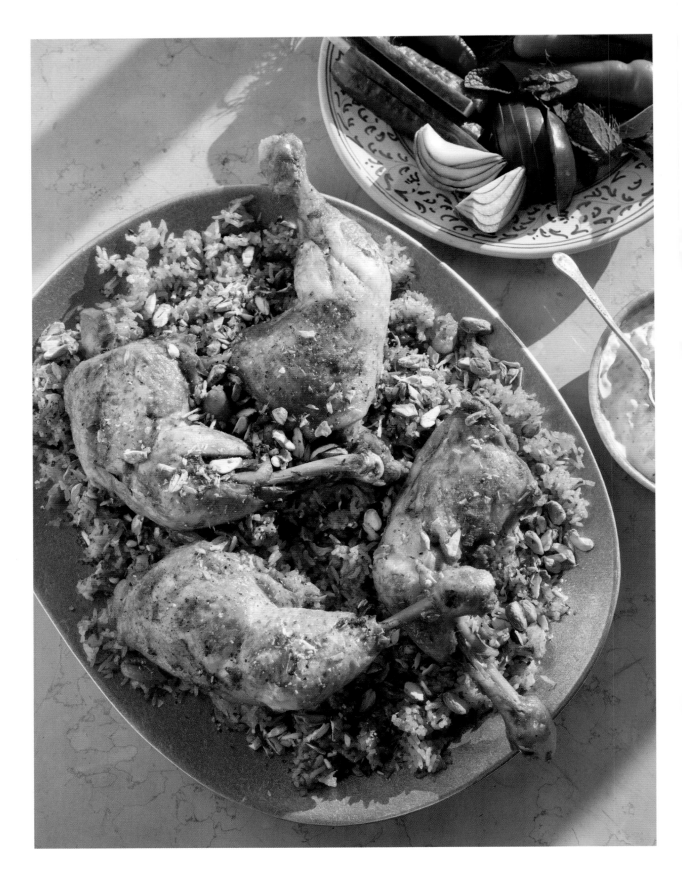

KABSA RICE WITH CHICKEN

TO MAKE

✧ ✧ ✧ ✧ ✧ ✧ ✧ ✧ ✧ ✧ ✧ ✧ ✧ ✧ ✧ ✧ ✧ ✧ ✧ ✧

2 tablespoons olive oil

4 chicken legs

1 tablespoon cumin seeds

3 cloves

1 cinnamon stick

3 green cardamom pods

1½ tablespoons kabsa spice
   mix (page 32)

1½ teaspoons baharat (page 32)

1 teaspoon ground black pepper

1 bay leaf

1 large onion, finely chopped

1 green pepper, deseeded and
   finely chopped

1 or 2 small red chiles (optional)

1 x 14 oz (400 g) can of tomatoes

2 teaspoons salt

2 cups (400 g) American golden
   rice (or other long-grain rice)

½ cup (75 g) raisins or golden
   raisins

Heat the olive oil in a large, heavy-based pot over medium-high heat, add the chicken legs skin side down and brown for about 7 minutes (you may need to do this in 2 batches). Remove and set aside on a plate.

Put the cumin seeds in the same pot and toast for a minute then add all the remaining spices and the bay leaf, and cook for a further minute, stirring continuously. Add the onion and green pepper and fry for 10 minutes until soft, stirring regularly and turning the heat down if needed to ensure the spices don't catch. If you want to add a chile or two, slice in half lengthways, and add to the pot.

Add the tomatoes and salt, fill the empty tomato can with water and pour it in, then bring everything up to a boil. Add the chicken back in, making sure it's completely submerged in the sauce; if it's not, just top up with a little more water. Put the lid on and turn down to a bubbling simmer for 45 minutes.

Meanwhile, wash the rice in a sieve until the water runs clear, then place it in a bowl with enough water to cover. Soak for 30 minutes.

Heat your broiler.

Transfer the chicken from the pot to a low-sided roasting pan. Taste the sauce at this point, making sure the seasoning is right.

Drain the rice and stir it into the pot along with the raisins, making sure you have about ¾ in (2 cm) of liquid above the rice; if not add a little more water.

Bring the rice back up to a boil, then put the lid on and immediately turn it right down to the lowest simmer for 15 minutes. Take off the heat, leaving the lid tightly on, and rest for 10 minutes.

While the rice is resting, place the chicken under the broiler for 5–10 minutes until the skin crisps up again and is golden.

TO SERVE

✧ ✧ ✧ ✧ ✧ ✧ ✧ ✧ ✧ ✧ ✧ ✧ ✧ ✧ ✧ ✧ ✧ ✧ ✧ ✧

Shelled pistachios (optional)

⅓ cup (50 g) pine nuts, toasted

Handful of chopped parsley

Laban bi khiar (page 97)

Green salad

Lift the lid on the rice and stir the rice gently with a fork to break up the grains, then serve with the chicken, pistchios, if using, pine nuts, parsley, laban bi khiar, and a green salad.

KABSA RICE WITH VEGETABLES

TO MAKE

✤ ✤ ✤ ✤ ✤ ✤ ✤ ✤ ✤ ✤ ✤ ✤ ✤ ✤ ✤ ✤ ✤ ✤

¼ cup (60 ml) olive oil

1 tablespoon cumin seeds

9 oz (250 g) chestnut
  mushrooms, sliced

3 red peppers, deseeded and
  roughly chopped

1 green pepper, deseeded
  and finely chopped

2 red onions, cut into
  slices ½ in (1 cm) thick

1 or 2 small red chiles (optional)

1½ tablespoons kabsa spice
  (page 32)

1 teaspoon ground black pepper

1½ teaspoons baharat (page 32)

3 cloves

1 cinnamon stick

3 green cardamom pods

1 bay leaf

2 teaspoons salt

1 x 14 oz (400 g) can of tomatoes

2 cups (400 g) American golden
  rice (or other long-grain rice)

½ cup (75 g) raisins or golden
  raisins

Heat 2 tablespoons of the olive oil in a large heavy-based pot
over medium-high heat, then add the cumin seeds and toast for
a minute, followed by the sliced mushrooms. Cook over high heat
for 4–5 minutes, stirring occasionally. Remove from the pot once
they are nice and golden and set aside on a plate.

Add the remaining olive oil to the pot and cook the peppers and
red onions for 8–10 minutes, to get a little color. If you want to add a
chile or two, slice in half lengthways and add to the pot. Return the
mushrooms to the pot with spices and salt. Fry for 2–3 minutes then
add the tomatoes.

Fill the empty tomato can with water and add it in, then bring
everything up to a boil. Put the lid on and turn down to a bubbling
simmer for 25–30 minutes.

Meanwhile, wash the rice in a sieve until the water runs clear, then
place in a bowl with enough water to cover. Soak for 30 minutes.

Taste the sauce at this point, making sure the seasoning is right,
then drain the rice and stir it into the pot, along with the raisins.

Bring the rice back up to a boil, then put the lid on and immediately
turn it right down to the lowest simmer for 15 minutes. Take off the
heat, leaving the lid tightly on, and rest for 10 minutes.

TO SERVE

✤ ✤ ✤ ✤ ✤ ✤ ✤ ✤ ✤ ✤ ✤ ✤ ✤ ✤ ✤ ✤ ✤

Laban bi khiar (page 97)

⅓ cup (50 g) pine nuts, toasted

Handful of chopped parsley

Green salad

Lift the lid on the rice and stir the rice gently with a fork to break up
the grains, then serve with the laban bi khiar, pine nuts, parsley,
and a green salad.

STUFFED ZUCCHINIS, EGGPLANTS, AND PEPPERS

If you can't find high-fat ground lamb, add 1 tablespoon of ghee.

PREPARE THE VEGETABLES

❖ ❖ ❖ ❖ ❖ ❖ ❖ ❖ ❖ ❖ ❖ ❖ ❖ ❖ ❖ ❖ ❖

5 baby eggplants
10 baby zucchinis
4 peppers

Core the eggplants and zucchinis so you have a hole down the middle to stuff, then remove the stems from the peppers to reveal a hole, also for stuffing. Keep the pepper stems to use as lids.

FOR THE FILLING

❖ ❖ ❖ ❖ ❖ ❖ ❖ ❖ ❖ ❖ ❖ ❖ ❖ ❖ ❖ ❖ ❖

1 cup (200 g) short-grain
  Egyptian rice
2 tablespoons safflower
2 teaspoons ground cumin
1 teaspoon baharat (page 32)
14 oz (400 g) high-fat (30%)
  ground lamb
Salt and ground black pepper

For the filling, wash the rice until the water runs clear then add to a bowl with the safflower and mix thoroughly (wearing gloves to save your hands from turning yellow). Add the cumin, baharat, ground lamb, a good pinch of salt, and 1 teaspoon of black pepper, then mix again with your hands.

FOR THE SAUCE

❖ ❖ ❖ ❖ ❖ ❖ ❖ ❖ ❖ ❖ ❖ ❖ ❖ ❖ ❖ ❖ ❖

Juice of 1 lemon
2 quantities (scant 1 cup/200 ml)
  tamarind sauce (page 130)
10 garlic cloves, smashed into
  a paste
1 teaspoon baharat (page 32)
1 tablespoon safflower
2 tablespoons tomato paste
Salt and ground black pepper

For the sauce, combine the lemon juice, tamarind sauce, garlic, baharat, safflower, tomato paste, a good pinch of salt, and 1 teaspoon of black pepper in another bowl, and mix together.

Stuff the cavities of the vegetables until three-quarters full then stand them upright in a deep, 12 in (30 cm) diameter, heavy-based pot or Dutch oven, so they are tightly packed.

Pour over the sauce to just cover everything; you might not need all of it, so set aside the rest in case you need to top it up later. Tightly cover with foil or a lid and place over high heat until the liquid is boiling. Boil for 10 minutes, then turn the heat down to low and simmer for 1 hour before serving.

MY JOURNEY TO THE UK, PART 2

SO, HOW DID I FINALLY make it to the UK? I told the Home Office it was in the back of a truck, but the truth is I came with a fake ID on a first-class Eurostar ticket from Paris to London.

After the failure of the flights to Heathrow, I asked my contact for a new passport. This time he sent a genuine passport, but it wasn't my face on the photo. It was a man who looked only a little like me, but it would be good enough. I hoped. I didn't want to leave anything else to chance, I wanted to take control of the situation, so I decided I'd book my own ticket. There was no way I was going back to the airport so I headed to the train station. I'd take the Eurostar to London. When I got to Gare du Nord, it was early evening, rush hour, and there were no regular tickets left, only first class. It was expensive, €182, almost all the money I had left, but by then I had psyched myself up, I was ready. I was leaving tonight, no more waiting around. I bought the ticket and headed to security.

I swear I was visibly shaking as I approached French passport control. I handed my papers over and the officer looked at them, and then looked at me. And I could see at once in his eyes that he knew. He didn't believe the man in the photo was me, but he waved me through anyway. I didn't understand why, was it another miracle? But then I saw. Ahead of me was another checkpoint, the British one. I was shocked to see it; I didn't know they were both this side of the train. And I was so, so scared. Standing in the line, trying to figure out the situation and look calm, while panic was building inside me. The British passport officer was questioning the woman in front of me. Really interrogating her. Why was she in Paris? Why was she traveling alone? Where was she going in the UK? How long for? She was the most English-looking person I'd ever seen. If he was asking her so many questions, how was he going to react when it was my turn? Syrian, physically worn down after months on the road, with my smuggler's fake ID? Their voices continued to rise along with my anxiety, but then the woman suddenly exploded, screaming and swearing until security pulled her away. Now it was me.

I walked over to the desk and slid my ticket and passport under the glass. Behind the screen, the officer was talking to his colleague in the next booth, explaining what had just happened, still worked up from the woman's reaction. He scanned my passport in his machine without even looking at it, or me. In fact, he hadn't said a word to me at all. He was totally ignoring me. I thought to myself: what would a British person do? What would a British person, holding a first-class ticket do? I said,

168   MAINS

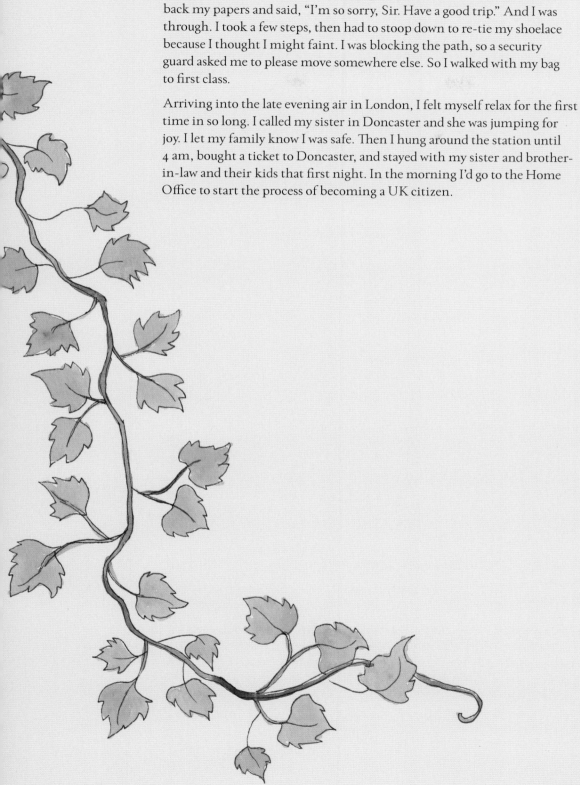

"Excuse me, I haven't got all day." Surprised and flustered he handed me back my papers and said, "I'm so sorry, Sir. Have a good trip." And I was through. I took a few steps, then had to stoop down to re-tie my shoelace because I thought I might faint. I was blocking the path, so a security guard asked me to please move somewhere else. So I walked with my bag to first class.

Arriving into the late evening air in London, I felt myself relax for the first time in so long. I called my sister in Doncaster and she was jumping for joy. I let my family know I was safe. Then I hung around the station until 4 am, bought a ticket to Doncaster, and stayed with my sister and brother-in-law and their kids that first night. In the morning I'd go to the Home Office to start the process of becoming a UK citizen.

BUTTERED HALIBUT

A beloved, traditional dish in Syria that's very popular in the summer, this recipe is particularly appreciated on the Mediterranean seaside. This dish is a real crowd-pleaser because of its simplicity; the sauce is only here to enhance the flavor of the halibut and the lemon brings enough acidity and freshness without overpowering it.

TO MAKE

❖ ❖ ❖ ❖ ❖ ❖ ❖ ❖ ❖ ❖ ❖ ❖ ❖ ❖ ❖ ❖ ❖ ❖

3½ tablespoons butter
2 garlic cloves, crushed
1 teaspoon cumin seeds
1 teaspoon salt
½ teaspoon ground black pepper
4 x 7 oz (200 g) halibut fillets
  (or other firm white fish fillets)
1 lemon, thinly sliced
Sprinkle of fresh thyme leaves
Sprinkle of sumac
Sprinkle of Aleppo chile flakes

Preheat the oven to 350°F (180°C).

In a small saucepan, melt the butter over a medium-low heat. Once melted, add the garlic, cumin, salt, and pepper, and stir to combine.

Put the fish fillets in a baking dish and pour on the butter mixture. Lay the lemon slices on top and cover the dish with foil. Bake for 5–8 minutes, depending on the thickness of the fillets, then remove the foil and bake for another 5 minutes until the fish flakes easily with a fork.

Sprinkle with a little thyme, sumac, and chile flakes and serve.

KUFTAH TAHINI

This recipe needs a high-fat ground beef, and works well with just ground lamb or just ground beef too, if you didn't want to do a mix.

Pictured overleaf.

FOR THE SAUCE

❖ ❖ ❖ ❖ ❖ ❖ ❖ ❖ ❖ ❖ ❖ ❖ ❖ ❖ ❖ ❖ ❖ ❖

1 onion, roughly chopped
3 garlic cloves, peeled
Small handful of parsley,
  stalks and leaves separated
1 tablespoon red pepper paste

For the sauce, in a blender, blend the onion, garlic, parsley stalks (reserve and chop the leaves for serving), and red pepper paste until smooth.

TO MAKE

❖ ❖ ❖ ❖ ❖ ❖ ❖ ❖ ❖ ❖ ❖ ❖ ❖ ❖ ❖ ❖ ❖ ❖

1 lb 10 oz (750 g) ground beef
  (15–20% fat)
9 oz (250 g) ground lamb
  (15–20% fat)
2 tablespoons Greek-style yogurt
2 tablespoons pomegranate
  molasses
1 teaspoon ground black pepper
1 teaspoon baharat (page 32)
½ teaspoon ground coriander
½ teaspoon ground cumin
2 teaspoons salt

Preheat the oven to 425°F (220°C).

Put the ground meats in a mixing bowl with the blended sauce, yogurt, pomegranate molasses, black pepper, baharat, ground coriander, cumin, and salt. Mix well with your hands until everything is combined.

Put the spiced meat in a 12 in (30 cm) round baking pan or ovenproof frying pan, and pat down with your hands into an even layer. With your fingertips, press down around the edges of the pan to separate the mixture from the edges of the pan a little. Again, with your fingertips, dimple the surface all over.

FOR THE GARNISH

✦ ✦ ✦ ✦ ✦ ✦ ✦ ✦ ✦ ✦ ✦ ✦ ✦ ✦ ✦ ✦ ✦

1 large tomato, cut into 6 wedges
1 red onion, cut into slices
   ½ in (1 cm) thick
2–3 red chiles, halved
   lengthways (optional)
1 teaspoon dried rosemary
1 tablespoon olive oil
Salt and ground black pepper

Arrange the fresh tomato wedges, red onion, chiles (if using), and dried rosemary on top, then drizzle with the olive oil and season with salt and pepper.

Bake in the oven for 30 minutes until crispy and golden on top. If there is any liquid that has come from the meat, drain it off and return to the oven to finish.

TO SERVE

✦ ✦ ✦ ✦ ✦ ✦ ✦ ✦ ✦ ✦ ✦ ✦ ✦ ✦ ✦ ✦ ✦

5 tablespoons tahini sauce
   (page 54)
Chile oil (optional)
Pita bread
Green plate (page 45)

While it is still hot, drizzle with the tahini sauce and chile oil (if using), and serve with the reserved chopped parsley leaves, pita bread, and green plate. I also love it in pita bread, like a sandwich.

KUFTAH BETINJAN

FOR THE TOMATO SAUCE

✧ ✧ ✧ ✧ ✧ ✧ ✧ ✧ ✧ ✧ ✧ ✧ ✧ ✧ ✧ ✧

1 x 14 oz (400 g) can of tomatoes
1 tablespoon tomato paste
Scant ½ cup (100 g) tamarind
   sauce (page 130)
1 garlic clove, peeled
½ teaspoon ground coriander
½ teaspoon ground cumin
1 teaspoon baharat (page 32)
½ teaspoon salt
1 teaspoon ground black pepper

In a food processor, blend all the ingredients for the tomato sauce together, then pour into a large bowl and set aside.

TO MAKE

✧ ✧ ✧ ✧ ✧ ✧ ✧ ✧ ✧ ✧ ✧ ✧ ✧ ✧ ✧ ✧

1 yellow onion, roughly chopped
1 small tomato, halved
1 lb 5 oz (600 g) ground lamb
1 teaspoon baharat (page 32)
½ teaspoon salt
½ teaspoon ground black pepper
6 baby eggplants, or
   1–2 medium-sized ones
1 red onion, peeled
2 large beefsteak tomatoes

In the same food processor (wash it first), process the yellow onion and small tomato and put it in another mixing bowl with the ground lamb, baharat, salt, and pepper. Use your hands to mix well to combine, then roll the mixture into 1 oz (25 g) balls (each about the size of a large walnut). Lightly flatten into discs.

Preheat the oven to 400°F (200°C).

Slice the eggplants ½ in (1 cm) thick (if using larger eggplants, cut them in half lengthways first). Cut the red onion in half through the root and the beefsteak tomatoes in half through the core. Cut each halved vegetable into half-moon slices ½ in (1 cm) thick. Arrange the lamb discs and the vegetables (skin side up) in a large ovenproof sauté pan or a baking dish about 10 in x 12 in (25 x 30 cm), alternating them as you go.

Pour on the tomato sauce then cover the dish with foil and bake in the oven for 20 minutes. Remove the foil and return to the oven for 25 minutes until the lamb is golden on top and the eggplants are soft.

TO SERVE

✧ ✧ ✧ ✧ ✧ ✧ ✧ ✧ ✧ ✧ ✧ ✧ ✧ ✧ ✧ ✧

Juice of 1 lemon
Chopped parsley
Cooked rice or bulgur
Green plate (page 45)

Squeeze the lemon juice on top and scatter with parsley to finish, then serve with rice or bulgur and a green plate.

MANZILAT BETINJAN

Baked eggplants and lamb

This is ideally made with baby eggplants, but I've adapted it here to use the larger ones. If you can find baby ones, I'd recommend using those instead — 6 – 8 of them.

TO MAKE

✧ ✧ ✧ ✧ ✧ ✧ ✧ ✧ ✧ ✧ ✧ ✧ ✧ ✧ ✧ ✧

3 eggplants
4 – 5 tablespoons olive oil
1 tablespoon cumin seeds
1 teaspoon baharat (page 32)
1 tablespoon ground black pepper
2 small onions, finely chopped
1 tablespoon tomato paste
1 lb 2 oz (500 g) ground lamb
    (15 – 20% fat)
3 large beefsteak or vine
    tomatoes (the best, reddest
    ones you can get), sliced
2 green peppers (ideally
    Turkish ones but you can
    use bell peppers), deseeded
    and finely sliced
Salt

Using a swivel vegetable peeler, peel off the skin from the eggplants in vertical stripes, so you're left with some skin on; this will give them a little more of a smoky taste. Now cut them across into round slices ½ in (1 cm) thick and place in a single layer on a few baking sheets. Salt them generously then lay some paper towels on top to soak up the moisture that will come out of them — this will take about 10 minutes. Replace the damp paper towels with new sheets to remove as much moisture as you can, patting them down. This is important as you want your eggplants to be as dry as possible.

Preheat the oven to 400°F (200°C).

Rub 2 – 3 tablespoons of olive oil all over the now-dry eggplant slices, then roast in the oven for 15 – 20 minutes until golden on top and slightly softened.

Meanwhile, put 2 tablespoons of olive oil in a large pan over medium heat. Add the cumin seeds, baharat, black pepper, and a sprinkle of salt and cook for a minute, then add the onions and gently fry for 5 minutes until they begin to soften. Now add the tomato paste and ground lamb and stir for 5 minutes. Remove the eggplants from the oven and layer them into a baking dish, about 8 by 12 in (30 x 20 cm). Spoon over the lamb, then lay on the sliced tomatoes, followed by the peppers. Place back in the oven for 20 minutes until slightly crisp on top.

TO SERVE

✧ ✧ ✧ ✧ ✧ ✧ ✧ ✧ ✧ ✧ ✧ ✧ ✧ ✧ ✧ ✧

Plain rice (page 48)
Green plate (page 45)

Serve straight away with plain rice and a green plate.

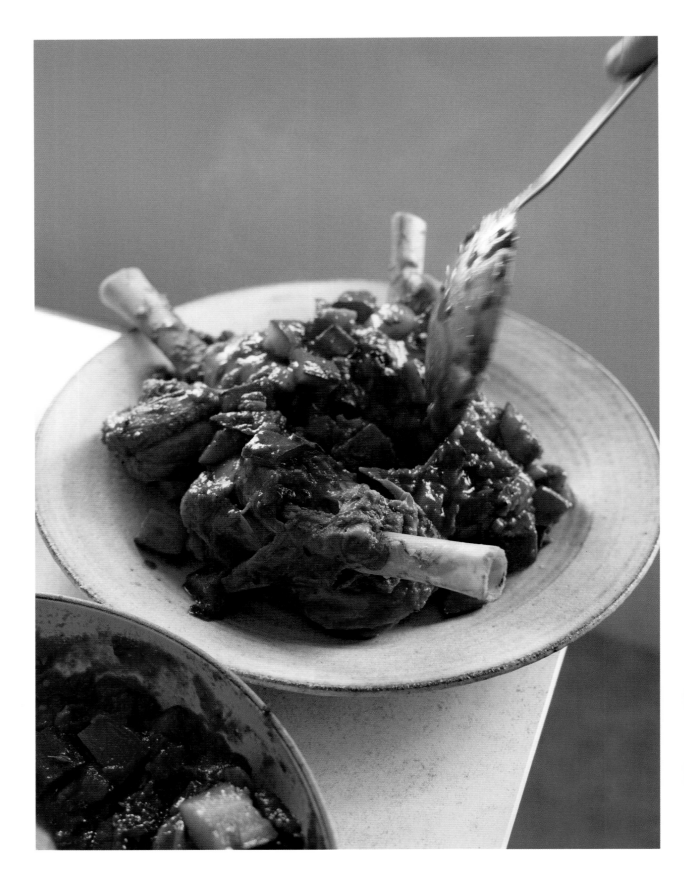

TABAKH ROHO

Tabakh roho means "to cook by itself" in Arabic. This makes a lot of delicious lamb stock; allow the leftover stock to cool completely and then store in the fridge for up to 4 days, or in the freezer for 3 months.

FOR THE LAMB

❖ ❖ ❖ ❖ ❖ ❖ ❖ ❖ ❖ ❖ ❖ ❖ ❖ ❖ ❖ ❖ ❖ ❖ ❖

4 lamb shanks
Choose any 2 – 3 herbs and
  spices from: fresh rosemary,
  fresh or dried bay leaves,
  fresh thyme, cloves, cardamom
  pods, cinnamon stick
1 whole garlic head, halved
  horizontally

Place the lamb shanks, chosen herbs and spices, and halved garlic head in a large pot and add enough water to cover everything. Bring to a boil, scooping off any scum that comes to the surface. Cover with a lid then turn down the heat to a low simmer for 1½ – 2 hours until the meat is about to fall off the bone (the longer you cook it, the more delicious it will be, so feel free to continue for a little longer). Take off the heat, transfer the shanks to a large bowl, and keep the lamb stock that's left over for later.

FOR THE SAUCE

❖ ❖ ❖ ❖ ❖ ❖ ❖ ❖ ❖ ❖ ❖ ❖ ❖ ❖ ❖ ❖ ❖ ❖ ❖

2 tablespoons olive oil
2 teaspoons cumin seeds
2 onions, roughly chopped
1 eggplant, peeled and
  cut into 1¼ in (3 cm) cubes
4 zucchinis, cut into ¾ in
  (2 cm) cubes
1 x 14 oz (400 g) can of chopped
  tomatoes
1 tablespoon tomato paste
Scant ½ cup (100 ml) tamarind
  sauce (page 130)
2 teaspoons baharat (page 32)
1 teaspoon ground black pepper
5 garlic cloves, crushed to a paste
3 teaspoons dried mint
Salt

Put the olive oil in another pot over medium heat, then add the cumin seeds and toast for a minute before adding the onions and salt to taste. Stir and cook for a few minutes, then add the eggplant cubes on top of the onions — do not stir!

Turn down the heat to low, cover, and allow everything to steam for 10 minutes before adding the zucchinis — again, without stirring. Cover again and continue to cook for 10 minutes. Now add the chopped tomatoes, tomato paste, tamarind sauce, a scant ½ cup (100 ml) of the reserved lamb stock, and the baharat, black pepper, and salt to taste.

Gently stir all your layers together and nestle in the lamb shanks. Put the crushed garlic in a small bowl with a few spoonfuls of the sauce and mix together, then add this to the pot. Simmer for 10 – 15 minutes, adding the dried mint in the last 5 minutes.

TO SERVE

❖ ❖ ❖ ❖ ❖ ❖ ❖ ❖ ❖ ❖ ❖ ❖ ❖ ❖ ❖ ❖ ❖ ❖ ❖

Plain bulgur (page 49)
Green plate (page 45)

Serve with plain bulgur and a green plate.

KIBBEH

Flat and baked

TO MAKE

✧ ✧ ✧ ✧ ✧ ✧ ✧ ✧ ✧ ✧ ✧ ✧ ✧ ✧ ✧ ✧

2 tablespoons olive oil

1 teaspoon cumin seeds

2 small onions, finely diced

5½ oz (150 g) ground lamb

2 teaspoons salt

2 teaspoons ground black pepper

2 teaspoons baharat (page 32)

⅓ cup (50 g) toasted pine nuts

5½ oz (150 g) lean (5% fat)
  ground beef

Grated zest of ½ lemon

Generous 1 cup (200 g) fine
  bulgur, rinsed and drained

2 tablespoons melted ghee

1 teaspoon safflower (optional)

Preheat the oven to 350°F (180°C).

Heat the olive oil in a frying pan over medium heat, add the cumin seeds, and toast for 30 seconds. Add half the onion and fry for 5–7 minutes or until softened but not colored. Add the ground lamb and 1 teaspoon each of the salt, pepper, and baharat and fry for 4–5 minutes. Once the meat is cooked, add the pine nuts, remove from the heat, and put to one side to cool.

Put the remaining onion in a meat grinder or food processor with the ground beef, lemon zest, and remaining salt, pepper, and baharat and grind. Thoroughly drain the bulgur and add it to the grinder or processor and grind again until smooth; you want the paste to be as smooth as possible with no visible onion or bulgur. If necessary, add a tablespoon of water to help combine, then grind.

Brush an 8 in (20 cm) square baking pan or sheet with 1 tablespoon of the melted ghee. Add half of the beef mixture to cover the base of the pan and pat down with the back of a spoon or spatula until flattened. Tip the lamb mixture in an even layer on top of the beef, followed by the remaining beef mixture. Smooth the top then cut into 16 squares. Brush the top with the remaining ghee, sprinkle with safflower, if using, and bake for 35–40 minutes until starting to brown on top.

TO SERVE

✧ ✧ ✧ ✧ ✧ ✧ ✧ ✧ ✧ ✧ ✧ ✧ ✧ ✧ ✧ ✧

Green plate (page 45)

Serve straight away, with a green plate.

KIBBEH MEQLIA

Rolled and fried

TO MAKE

❖ ❖ ❖ ❖ ❖ ❖ ❖ ❖ ❖ ❖ ❖ ❖ ❖ ❖ ❖ ❖ ❖

1 quantity of beef and lamb
   kibbeh mixtures (page 182)
4¼ cups (1 liter) vegetable oil,
   for deep-frying

Prepare the lamb and beef and bulgur mixtures as directed on page 182.

Roll the bulgur mixture into large golf-ball-sized balls, then, wetting your thumb and palm a little, make a dent in the middle of each ball using your thumb. Now, with the ball in one hand, work your way around the edges of the hole to start to make it larger, turning as you go to form a cup. You might find it easier to use both index fingers here. Have a little bowl of water ready and remember to wet your hands as you go, as this will stop everything from sticking. The thinner you can get the shell, the better. But it will take practice, so keep going.

Once your little cup is ready, add a small tablespoon of the lamb mixture inside. Then, holding the ball in one hand, seal up the top into a rugby ball shape, making sure there are no gaps. They don't have to be a perfect shape, just well sealed so that when you fry, no filling comes out. Repeat with all the remaining balls.

Heat the oil in a heavy-based pot, making sure it comes no more than halfway up the sides of the pot, and heat to 350°F/180°C (test it is ready by dropping a little of the mixture into the oil; if it floats and bubbles, then you are ready to go). Deep-fry the kibbeh in small batches for 3–4 minutes, turning so they are golden brown all over. Drain on paper towels.

TO SERVE

❖ ❖ ❖ ❖ ❖ ❖ ❖ ❖ ❖ ❖ ❖ ❖ ❖ ❖ ❖ ❖ ❖

Green plate (page 45)

Serve immediately, with a green plate.

MAKLOUBEH

Lamb and rice

If your butcher can't give you finely diced lamb shoulder, then ground lamb works fine here.

TO MAKE

❖ ❖ ❖ ❖ ❖ ❖ ❖ ❖ ❖ ❖ ❖ ❖ ❖ ❖ ❖ ❖ ❖ ❖

1¾ cups (350 g) long-grain rice
3 large eggplants, sliced
   lengthways, ½ in (1 cm) thick
2 tablespoons olive oil
1 tablespoon ghee
1 teaspoon cumin seeds
12 oz (350 g) finely diced lamb
   shoulder (get your butcher to
   do this)
1½ teaspoons baharat (page 32)
2¾ cups (650 ml) water
Salt and ground black pepper

Preheat the oven to 400°F (200°C).

Wash the rice until the water runs clear, then soak in a bowl of cold water for 30 minutes.

Meanwhile, lay the eggplant slices on a few baking sheets in a single layer. Brush each slice with olive oil and sprinkle over a good pinch each of salt and pepper. Roast in the oven for 15–20 minutes until soft and lightly golden, then remove and allow to cool slightly.

Put the ghee and cumin seeds in a large 9 in (23 cm) diameter sauté pan and toast for a minute over medium-high heat. Now add the lamb and brown for 5 minutes. Add ½ teaspoon each of salt and pepper and ½ teaspoon of the baharat. Stir to coat the lamb in the spices, then pat it down so it's all in one layer. Take off the heat and let it cool a little.

Layer the roasted eggplant over the top of the lamb, with half the slices folded up the sides of the pan to line it, so the sides are completely covered (you're building a wall for the rice to cook inside).

Measure out the water into a jug and stir in the remaining teaspoon of baharat, 1 teaspoon of salt, and ½ teaspoon of black pepper.

Drain the rice then add it to the pan lined with eggplants. Flatten the rice into an even layer with the back of a spoon, then carefully pour the water into the spoon to direct the water gently, into the edges of the pan so that you don't disturb the layers.

Cover with a lid and bring everything to a slow boil over medium heat, then turn down to the lowest heat you can and gently simmer for 15 minutes. Take off the heat and leave to rest for 10 minutes.

TO SERVE

❖ ❖ ❖ ❖ ❖ ❖ ❖ ❖ ❖ ❖ ❖ ❖ ❖ ❖ ❖ ❖ ❖

Toasted pine nuts
Laban bi khiar (page 97)
Green salad
Small handful of parsley
   and/or mint leaves

To serve, remove the lid and place a large serving plate on top of the pan, then carefully but confidently flip the pan over and lift it little by little to reveal the makloubeh. Scatter with the pine nuts.

Serve with laban bi khiar, green salad, and fresh herbs.

FROM REFUGEE
TO UK CITIZEN

Being a refugee is exhausting. It's emotional. It's depressing. It involves so much waiting, unable to do anything, completely at the mercy of a constantly changing series of people who mostly don't seem to care. You rely on other people in a way you haven't had to before. You're totally powerless. Even the people involved in the process don't seem to understand the process, and in many ways it's not their fault because it truly makes no sense. There doesn't seem to be any logic to how any of it works.

The day after I arrived in the UK, I walked into the Home Office in Leeds and simply said, "Hello, I'm a Syrian refugee. I came here illegally; will you please take me in?" The man behind the desk gave me a phone number to call. It was all so incredibly routine for them, no one seemed surprised I was there. The woman I spoke to on the phone took my number and I gave her my brother-in-law's number too. She asked if I had somewhere to stay and I said I was staying with family. She then said they'd be in touch about the next steps in getting my status as an asylum seeker approved. And that was it.

After that initial brief phone conversation in Leeds, it was 27 days until I was contacted again. And in that time, no one checked my background, they didn't verify any of my details, they didn't call me to make sure I was still where I said I was. I could have been a murderer. I couldn't believe it really: here I was telling them I was in this country illegally and no one even wanted to make sure I wasn't a criminal.

A month later I was back in London. More basic questions. They took my fingerprints, photos. They asked me why we didn't just say no to Assad, why we didn't stand up to him. They didn't seem to know anything about what was really going on over there. I am a father with three daughters; you can't just say no to a dictator. You would be killed. They asked me why my wife's last name was different to mine. In Syria, women keep their names when they marry, but they made me feel like I was trying to hide something.

And then it was another three months, no contact again, while I waited for my second interview. How can a person live in a new country for months and months with no support and unable to work? I was lucky I had my family who were happy to help, but I wanted to support myself. As a refugee you cannot work; even fully trained doctors cannot work, and we need them here! Officially, you are entitled to a small amount of money each week from the government, but it's nowhere near enough to live on, and every time I called, I was told it was "in process."

And as I quickly found out, people are very happy to take advantage of the desperation of asylum seekers.

That's when I moved down closer to London and found work in a carwash. I didn't want to work illegally, but months and months of doing nothing is hard. It's hard for someone like me, who has always supported themself, to have to depend so much on others. And it is very difficult mentally, to be in limbo, to be constantly wondering, what's next? What is happening? Has something gone wrong? You can get lost inside your own head. I always try to look for the good in any experience I have, but to be honest there wasn't a lot of good to be found at that time. I was treated badly at the carwash, I was underpaid, I slept in a portacabin. I was there 24 hours a day. People exploit other people in vulnerable situations, but I didn't really have a choice.

But April 26, 2016, six months after I had arrived in the UK, was a good day: my asylum seeker status was finally approved, which meant I was able to work legally. Even better, it meant I could submit my family reunion application and I started to let myself look forward to seeing my wife and daughters again. For some people, it can take a year for their application to be processed, but this time I was very lucky and in just three months, it had been granted.

Reuniting with my family in July 2016 was one of the most incredible moments of my life. It was something we had all been dreaming about, but hadn't wanted to hope for in case it took much longer than we expected, or didn't happen at all. The Home Office then granted us five years leave to remain in the UK, meaning we could live here for five years before applying for indefinite leave to remain. But after one year, you can apply for your UK citizenship. It costs a lot of money and involves a lot of stupid tests to "prove" your knowledge of life as a British citizen. Questions about its history, laws, and customs. Questions like "who won an Olympic gold for swimming in the 1970s?" Questions I'm sure many life-long British citizens would not know the answer to. But at midnight, exactly one year after we received our leave to remain, we sent in our applications for citizenship. We were ready and prepared, we had done all we could. What we weren't prepared for was the waiting that followed.

With my mother passing, my father had somehow been left behind and I knew I had to find a way to bring him over too. The Home Office rejected him as part of my family reunion application, because they said he wasn't family . . . My back and forth with them went on for a long time and ended in me taking them to court. I said I'd sponsor a visa for him, that I didn't need anything from the Home Office, I just wanted him to be with us. And in March 2018 he joined us in the UK, living between my sister's family and mine.

For many people I knew, their citizenship application took a few weeks to be approved, maybe a couple of months. We waited eleven long months with no updates. Waiting, waiting. Is there something wrong with my papers? Are they investigating something? I had a parking ticket, would that mean they'd send me back to Syria? Why does this person have their citizenship after just six weeks and we haven't? Then came the rumors that they'd be changing the citizenship laws soon. And then the Home Secretary revealed plans to send asylum seekers to Rwanda. Would we be among them? Even though we were so far in to the process? So much worry, so much uncertainty, so much anxiety. And every time I called, I was told "it's in process; it's still being processed."

We were now in 2022, so by this stage I was running a successful restaurant, employing people, my wife ran a catering company, we were paying taxes, my children were in school. What did we do? What more could we do?

And then, in December 2022, we finally received our official British citizenship.

I literally cannot describe what that meant to us. It was a very, very emotional moment for me. I had been dreaming of this moment for years, to belong somewhere fully again. You don't have to have British citizenship in order to be a Londoner, and I don't have any more loyalty to my new city because I am now a legal citizen. For me, I was accepted into this country when the people welcomed me in. When they tried my food and enjoyed it. When they hugged me in the street, followed my story on Instagram, when they told me gently that they were happy I was here. That was when I honestly felt like I was part of something again, when I had a home. I had my own citizenship a long time before it was granted by the Home Office, but we couldn't be deported now. We were safe.

MOUSSAKA

This is a Syrian version, and although it's called moussaka, it's not the one everyone will know. It's vegan, and a classic dish to be eaten during Christian fasting times. In Syria we deep-fry the eggplants, but I've adapted this recipe to be a little lighter, easier, and a little less greasy.

TO MAKE

✧ ✧ ✧ ✧ ✧ ✧ ✧ ✧ ✧ ✧ ✧ ✧ ✧ ✧ ✧ ✧

3 eggplants
2 – 3 tablespoons olive oil
Salt

Using a vegetable peeler, peel off the skin from the eggplants in vertical stripes, so you're left with some skin on; this will give them more of a smoky taste. Now cut them lengthways into slices ¾ in (2 cm) thick.

Arrange the eggplant slices in a single layer on a few baking sheets, salt them generously, then lay over some paper towels to soak up the moisture that will come out of them — this will take about 10 minutes. Replace the damp paper towels with fresh dry ones to remove as much moisture as you can, patting them all down. This is important as you want your eggplants to be as dry as possible so you won't have a soggy moussaka.

Preheat the oven to 400°F (200°C). Add the olive oil to the now-dry eggplants, rub it all over them, then roast in the oven for 15 minutes until golden.

FOR THE SAUCE

✧ ✧ ✧ ✧ ✧ ✧ ✧ ✧ ✧ ✧ ✧ ✧ ✧ ✧ ✧ ✧

3 tablespoons olive oil
1 teaspoon cumin seeds
5 garlic cloves, very finely sliced
1 tablespoon tomato paste
2 x 14 oz (400 g) cans of
    tomatoes
1 teaspoon ground black pepper
2 long green peppers
    or bell peppers, deseeded
    and finely sliced

Meanwhile, for the sauce, put 2 tablespoons of the olive oil in a large pot over medium heat. Add the cumin seeds and toast for a minute, then add the garlic and tomato paste for a few minutes to cook out. Now add the canned tomatoes and black pepper and simmer for 5 minutes.

Remove the eggplants from the oven and layer them all into a 12 x 8 in (30 x 20 cm) baking dish. Pour over the tomato sauce, followed by the sliced green peppers and a little more olive oil. Return to the oven for another 30 minutes. We don't want to cook the peppers through here; they are supposed to still have a little bite, so don't worry if they aren't soft.

TO SERVE

✧ ✧ ✧ ✧ ✧ ✧ ✧ ✧ ✧ ✧ ✧ ✧ ✧ ✧ ✧ ✧

Small handful of parsley,
    finely chopped
Plain bulgur (page 49)
Pickles
Green plate (page 45)

Finish with chopped parsley and serve with bulgur and pickles. This dish is most definitely served with a green plate.

FILO RICE

TO MAKE

✦ ✦ ✦ ✦ ✦ ✦ ✦ ✦ ✦ ✦ ✦ ✦ ✦ ✦ ✦ ✦ ✦ ✦

1 lb (450 g) diced lamb leg
2 bay leaves
3 cardamom pods
2 cloves
1 cup (200 g) long-grain rice
1 teaspoon cumin seeds
2 tablespoons olive oil
Pinch of salt
½ teaspoon ground cardamom
½ teaspoon ground ginger
1 teaspoon baharat (page 32)
1½ cups (200 g) frozen peas
¼ cup (40 g) pine nuts, toasted
⅓ cup (40 g) cashews, toasted
  and roughly chopped
½ teaspoon ground black pepper
1 package of filo pastry
¼ cup (60 ml) melted ghee

Put the lamb in a large pot with enough water to cover (about 4¼ cups/ 1 liter) and bring to a boil over high heat. Once it starts to boil, you'll see a foamy layer rise to the surface; remove this with a spoon. Once all the foam has been removed, add the bay leaves, cardamom pods, and cloves and turn down to a simmer. Cover with a lid and cook for 45–60 minutes until soft. Drain the lamb, keeping the cooking liquid.

Meanwhile, wash the rice until the water runs clear, soak in a bowl of cold water for 30 minutes, then drain.

In a pot over medium-high heat, toast the cumin seeds in the olive oil for a minute, then add the drained rice, salt, and ground spices to the pot and cover with an equal mixture of reserved lamb cooking water and water; the liquid should come about ½ in (1 cm) above the rice. Cover and increase the heat to a boil, then immediately turn down to a very low simmer for 15 minutes. Take off the heat and leave for 5 minutes. Separate the rice with a fork and transfer to a tray to cool evenly.

Once everything is cooled, mix together the lamb, rice, peas, nuts, and black pepper. Set aside.

Unroll your filo pastry and cover with a tea towel (this is important as you don't want the filo pastry to dry out).

Preheat the oven to 400°F (200°C). Brush some melted ghee into a low-sided roasting pan, to grease it.

Take one sheet of filo and fold in half and then in half again, so you have 4 layers (you can layer sheets if your sheets are smaller). Press the filo into a 4 in (10 cm) ramekin dish so it molds into the shape, but make sure you have an overhang to be able to fold over the top of the filling later. Fill the filo with rice and lamb mixture and fold the filo over the mixture to close it up.

Working quickly, put a hand over the closed filo and ramekin and flip it over onto the ghee-lined pan, so you have an upside-down parcel. Brush generously with ghee and repeat with the remaining rice and filo to make 5 more.

Bake for 30–35 minutes until the filo is golden all over.

TO SERVE

✦ ✦ ✦ ✦ ✦ ✦ ✦ ✦ ✦ ✦ ✦ ✦ ✦ ✦ ✦ ✦ ✦ ✦

Laban bi khiar (page 97)
Green salad

Remove from the oven and serve with laban bi khiar or green salad.

FUL MUDAMIS

Fava beans

You can find canned fava beans in most supermarkets.

FOR THE GREEN PASTE

✤ ✤ ✤ ✤ ✤ ✤ ✤ ✤ ✤ ✤ ✤ ✤ ✤ ✤ ✤ ✤ ✤ ✤

3 garlic cloves
1 green chile
Bunch of parsley, stalks only
  (save the leaves for serving)
Juice of 2 lemons
1 teaspoon ground cumin
½ teaspoon salt
2 tablespoons olive oil

Make the green paste by adding all the ingredients to a food processor and pulsing briefly, so it's still a little chunky.

TO MAKE

✤ ✤ ✤ ✤ ✤ ✤ ✤ ✤ ✤ ✤ ✤ ✤ ✤ ✤ ✤ ✤ ✤ ✤

1 cup (200 g) dried whole fava
  beans (or you can use 1 x 20 oz/
  570 g can fava beans, or canned
  chickpeas work well instead)
6⅓ cups (1.5 liters) water
½ teaspoon baking soda
Small bunch of parsley, leaves only
Small bunch of mint, leaves only
1 beefsteak tomato or 3 vine
  tomatoes, cut into ½ in
  (1 cm) cubes
½ red onion, finely diced
2 tablespoons extra virgin olive oil
Salt and ground black pepper

Soak the dried beans overnight in plenty of water. Drain and place in a pot with the measured water. Add the baking soda, bring to a boil, then simmer for 90 minutes, or until softened.

Drain the beans (if using canned, warm the beans through first) into a bowl and add the green sauce along with the herb leaves, tomato, onion, and extra virgin olive oil. Season with salt and pepper and stir together to combine.

TO SERVE

✤ ✤ ✤ ✤ ✤ ✤ ✤ ✤ ✤ ✤ ✤ ✤ ✤ ✤ ✤ ✤ ✤ ✤

Hummus (page 68)
Flatbread
Chile peppers, chopped
Laban bi khiar (page 97)

I love this served with hummus, flatbread, and chiles, but it's also delicious with laban bi khiar.

BURGHUL BI KUSA

Bulgur with zucchini

TO MAKE

✤ ✤ ✤ ✤ ✤ ✤ ✤ ✤ ✤ ✤ ✤ ✤ ✤ ✤ ✤ ✤ ✤

Scant ½ cup (100 ml) extra
  virgin olive oil
1 teaspoon cumin seeds
2 red onions, finely chopped
½ teaspoon ground cumin
1 teaspoon baharat (page 32)
Pinch of salt
½ teaspoon freshly ground
  black pepper
4 zucchinis, cut into ¾ in
  (2 cm) chunks
Small bunch of dill, chopped
Small bunch of cilantro, chopped
5 garlic cloves, crushed to a paste
2 cups (300 g) coarse bulgur

Put half the oil in a pot over medium heat, then add the cumin seeds
and toast for a minute. Add the chopped onions with the ground
cumin, baharat, salt, and pepper, then stir to coat in the oil. Cook
for 5–6 minutes until soft.

Add the zucchinis to the pot with the onions and spices.
Stir and cook for a further 5–6 minutes until the zucchinis
are slightly softened.

Stir in the chopped dill, cilantro, and crushed garlic and mix
it all together so everything is coated. Now add the bulgur and the
remaining oil. Add in enough water to cover the bulgur and zucchinis
(about ½ in/1 cm above everything), bring to a boil, then lower the
heat to its lowest for 5–6 minutes. Take off the heat and allow it to
sit, covered with a lid, for 2 minutes. When you lift the lid the bulgur
will be perfectly cooked, so just break up the grains with a fork.

TO SERVE

✤ ✤ ✤ ✤ ✤ ✤ ✤ ✤ ✤ ✤ ✤ ✤ ✤ ✤ ✤ ✤ ✤

Laban bi khiar (page 97)
Green salad

Serve with laban bi khiar and a green salad.

FIVE

DESSERTS

FIVE

DESSERTS

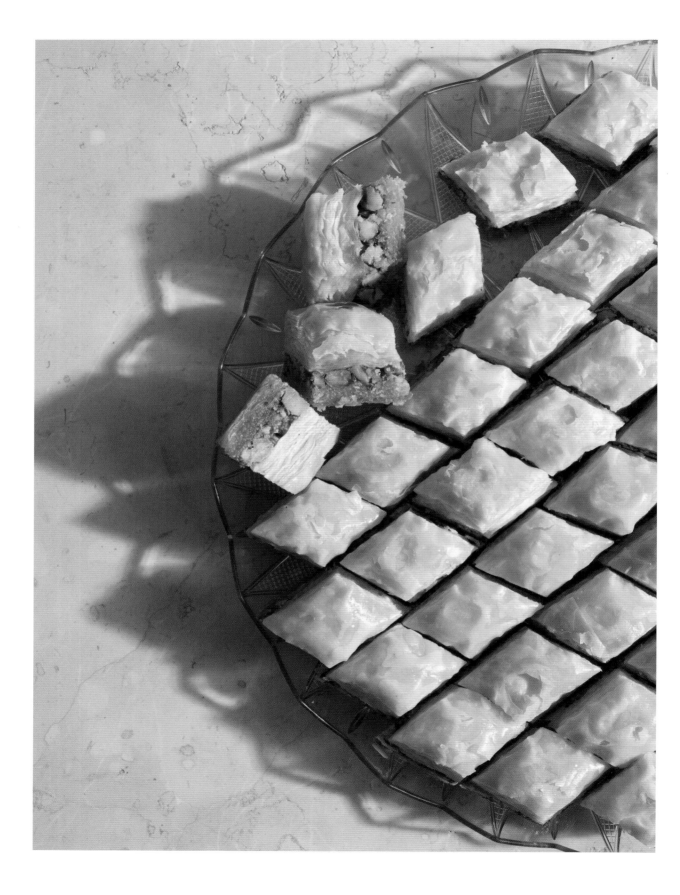

BAKLAWA

This recipe won't work with standard filo pastry, as it's too thick; you need to get the proper filo for baklawa that you'll find in Middle Eastern grocery stores.

The trick to good baklawa is to be quick and careful. Get everything ready around you before you start, including a large, clean tea towel to keep the filo from drying out while you're making it. This is a pistachio and walnut version, but you can use any nuts you like. I like to use a mix.

TO MAKE

❖ ❖ ❖ ❖ ❖ ❖ ❖ ❖ ❖ ❖ ❖ ❖ ❖ ❖ ❖ ❖

¾ cup (150 g) shelled pistachios
¾ cup (150 g) walnuts
1 teaspoon sugar
1 teaspoon orange blossom water
1 teaspoon water
Scant ½ cup (100 g) good-
   quality ghee, plus extra for
   greasing
1 lb (480 g) Turkish, extra-thin
   filo pastry

Preheat the oven to 340°F (170°C).

Start by toasting the nuts in a large baking pan in a single layer in the oven for 5 minutes. Remove and allow to cool. Sprinkle on the sugar, orange blossom water, and water, then crush the nuts either using a mortar and pestle or a blender. Be careful if using a blender; you want a very chunky texture, not a fine crumb. The water and sugar should make your nuts delicious and sticky.

Melt the ghee in a saucepan over low heat and set aside to stay warm. Brush a 14 x 10 in (35 x 25 cm) baking pan (with sides) with a little of the melted ghee.

Unroll the filo it so it's flat on the work surface, then lay the prepared baking pan on top of the filo and cut around the edge, so your filo is the exact same size. Remove the excess edges (use in another recipe), then place the cut filo in a clean tea towel to keep it from drying out (you should have at 24 layers of filo).

Place half the filo layers in the greased pan, then sprinkle all of the nuts on top. Spread them out into an even layer and pat them down a little. Now top with the other half of the filo layers, and, with the back of a spoon, tuck in the edges of the filo, so that they curl in neatly down the sides of the pan. Working quickly so the filo doesn't dry out, slice your baklawa into diamonds. I prefer them small, and make 40, but you can choose any size you like here.

If your ghee has cooled, reheat it again to melt, pour it over everything, then bake in the oven for 35 – 40 minutes until golden on top.

CONTINUED OVERLEAF

FOR THE SYRUP

✧ ✧ ✧ ✧ ✧ ✧ ✧ ✧ ✧ ✧ ✧ ✧ ✧ ✧ ✧ ✧ ✧ ✧

2½ cups (500 g) sugar
1⅔ cups (400 ml) water
1 slice of lemon
3 cardamom pods
1 cinnamon stick
1 teaspoon orange blossom water

While it's baking, make your syrup. Put the sugar and water in a heavy-based saucepan over medium heat and stir well until the sugar has dissolved. Add the lemon slice, cardamom, and cinnamon, then bring to a boil. Turn down to a gentle simmer for 5 minutes, then take off the heat and stir in the orange blossom water. Remove the cardamom and cinnamon.

Remove the baklawa from the oven then drain any excess ghee from the bottom. I do this by placing a clean tray on top of the baked baklawa and tipping it carefully so the ghee pours out from the bottom corner into a bowl (you can use this ghee for your next baklawa).

Now pour over your hot sugar syrup, one ladleful at a time, since you might not use it all. It's important that it's hot here; it should sizzle a bit when it's poured over. Continue to spoon over the syrup until it comes halfway up the baklawa. Allow to sit for a minute then drain off the excess syrup, the same way you did the ghee.

Serve hot or allow to cool then cover with foil.

ROLLED BAKLAWA

This is a variation on traditional baklawa.

Pictured overleaf.

TO MAKE

❖ ❖ ❖ ❖ ❖ ❖ ❖ ❖ ❖ ❖ ❖ ❖ ❖ ❖ ❖ ❖ ❖ ❖ ❖

¾ cup (150 g) shelled pistachios
¾ cup (150 g) walnuts
1 teaspoon sugar
1 teaspoon orange blossom water
1 teaspoon water
⅔ cup (150 g) good-quality ghee, melted
9½ oz (270 g) Turkish, extra-thin filo pastry
1 quantity syrup (see opposite)

Preheat the oven to 340°F (170°C).

Follow the steps as for the main baklawa recipe on page 205 to toast and grind the nuts with the sugar, orange blossom water, and water, and grease the baking pan with melted ghee.

Take 2 sheets of filo and place them one on top of the other lengthways in front of you. Scatter a heaped tablespoon of nuts over the filo sheet, then place a long skewer vertically in the middle of the filo sheet. Fold the sheet over, then roll it up, using the skewer to help. Lift the roll into the pan and then push the nut-filled filo off the skewer so it ruffles in the pan. Make sure the rolls lay flat in the pan.

Repeat with all the filo and nuts until the pan is neatly filled with the ruffled rolls.

Working quickly so the filo doesn't dry out, slice each rolled length into 6–8 pieces. I prefer them this smaller size, but you can choose any size you like here.

Pour the melted ghee over everything then bake in the oven for 35–40 minutes until golden on top.

While they are baking, make your sugar syrup following the instructions opposite.

Remove the baklawa from the oven then drain any excess ghee from the bottom (see opposite). Pour over your hot sugar syrup (see opposite).

Serve hot or allow to cool, then cover with foil.

ANGELS

MY WHOLE LIFE, I have been surrounded by angels. Despite everything I have been through, everything I have seen, I know I am one of the lucky ones. I've always felt as though when I've needed help the most, someone has been there for me. And that is why I always try to be there for the people around me too.

I struggled so much on my journey from Syria. It was the hardest thing I've ever done in my life. Crossing from Turkey in the boat, landing on the Greek coast, I was completely shattered from the inside. We were cold, exhausted, afraid of what came next, wearing our orange life jackets, and holding onto our few possessions, the only things left that told anything about who we really were. But then we looked up and saw an older lady waving and shouting down to us from the small cliff above the beach, "You are safe now, don't be scared!" And in that moment, I was so relieved. When I looked at her face, she looked so happy. Happier than I felt right then, even though I was in Europe, finally. She was jumping around all over the place wanting to help everyone, to reach us, to let us know we'd be OK now. We took photos together, but I was so overwhelmed, I wasn't able to thank her properly. And then just as she had arrived, she disappeared. It took a few hours for us all to figure out what was going to happen next and in that time I spoke to a volunteer doctor, helping translate for a pregnant woman who had been on our boat. I asked about the woman who had been waving to us and was told she was Norwegian, that she'd used her vacation from work to help refugees as they arrived in Greece. She was actually on her way back to the airport now, back to Norway, but had seen our boat coming in and wanted to come down to greet us first. I am so frustrated that I don't know her name. I want to thank her so much for making us feel welcome, for making us feel human again.

⬥

ON THE TRAIN from Stuttgart, I had no idea what I was going to do when I arrived in Paris. I don't speak French and I had never been there before, I had no idea what to expect or where to go. I looked up and down the train carriage, trying to work out a plan, when I saw a man, minding his own business, reading the Quran in Arabic. I went over to him and explained my situation: that I had been traveling through illegally, I didn't know where I was going to in Paris, and I was so, so tired. I needed a mattress and a shower, and that I could pay. I asked if he knew of anywhere I'd be safe.

He asked me what kind of hotel I needed. And I replied the cheapest one! Anything would do. He said he knew someone who worked in a hotel near Gard de Nord, and that he'd come with me to help me find the hotel, to check I was OK. It was a stop beyond his journey, but he came with me anyway, and when we got to the reception he started speaking in French with his friend. They told me to go up to the room to see if I liked it and if I did, I could stay in it, I'd be safe. All I needed was a passport. I said I didn't need to go up, that I was sure it was perfect, but they insisted and I went up to drop off my bag. I was gone for no more than five minutes, but when I came back down the man on reception said my room had been paid for two nights by the man from the train, and also my dinner that evening. He had already left, so I couldn't thank him. I found out his name was Achmed and he was Algerian-French, but the hotelier didn't have his contact details.

You see how lucky I am? I only asked for an address of a hotel, but instead he insisted he came all the way with me, to ensure that I was safe inside the hotel. I will always be grateful to Achmed for helping a stranger who was in need.

✦

WHEN I ARRIVED IN CALAIS, I knew immediately that I couldn't stay in The Jungle. The local gendarme was trying to keep everyone in the camp so they could keep control over them, but to me it felt lawless. I didn't even go inside. When I arrived in the city it was late at night. I didn't know anyone. I was a refugee with a Syrian passport; I was too afraid to go to a hotel. Along the way you kept hearing stories of police beating people, and I was emotionally and mentally prepared to be scared. I was cold and alone and didn't know what to do. And then I saw some Sudanese people walking past and asked them if they knew where I could stay. They asked me if I was Syrian and then pointed me towards a church where they said some other Syrians were sleeping. The church was in a square, but when I got there, I couldn't see any Syrians, just a very blonde woman sitting on top of some mattresses. I introduced myself and started to explain my situation, and for ten minutes she interrogated me, asking more questions, checking out my story. She then told me that she was keeping the mattresses safe while the Syrian men who were camping here tried to cross The Channel. They'd be able to explain to me how it all worked, if they came back, if their attempt was unsuccessful. In the meantime I could stay, and if they returned I could tell them Frederike said I could stay. She left me on the church steps, but 15 minutes later returned with a jacket, a blanket, a pillow, some painkillers, and some muscle-relaxing cream because my back was in a lot of pain. And also, hot tea and dinner. You can't imagine how I felt!

Every single morning Frederike would go for a jog, running past the church. And every morning — she didn't miss one day for the 64 days I was there — she'd put a fresh pot of tea down for us with a note next to it written on a napkin that said "Have a great morning" with a smiley face, or "Have a great day." Always with a smiley face. She never forgot the tea and she never forgot the note. We are still in touch today, and in fact we're great friends. She's stayed with my family, and we've been to visit hers. She was there when we opened the restaurant.

✛

THEN THERE WERE TWO FRENCH WOMEN who were driving through Calais on their way back to Paris after a vacation in the UK. They wanted to find out more about the situation and found us at our church. We were cooking at the time. They asked if they could talk to us. "Of course! But first try our food!" "Before I try your food, can I take your photo?" "Yes!" They were so friendly, so interested in trying to understand the situation in Syria, the situation in Calais, what it meant to be here. We cooked mujadara (page 158) and they loved it, the spices, the flavors. We exchanged numbers, and then they left. When the gendarme kicked us off the church steps, one of the women called me and asked if we were OK, where we'd be going next. She said it was all over the French news that they were taking everyone to The Jungle. I told her I didn't feel safe in Calais anymore and that we were heading to Paris, back to the hotel I'd stayed in before. "No," she said. She'd meet me from my train and we could stay with her in her apartment. They emptied a room in their apartment and three of us, me and two friends, stayed there for 13 days. It was from her apartment that I left to get the Eurostar to London.

✛

WHEN MY FAMILY were able to join me in the UK, when the family reunion application had been approved, I could barely afford to live by myself, let alone support them. I had got them out of Syria to Lebanon, and the charity Choose Love helped with their plane tickets from Beirut to the UK. That was the beginning of a long relationship with that charity and its founder, Josie, whom I work with a lot today. My family and I moved to High Wycombe, and it was through the local community that I met Toni (who introduced me to Cook For Syria, see page 10) and her friend Stephanie, both of them true angels. Toni and Stephanie helped me find a house to rent for my family and taught me about the system so I could get my children registered in school. The house was a little bit depressing inside, dirty, in need of lots of repairs. But it was big enough and honestly, it was perfect; it was our first family home together where we would be safe. After I'd paid the first month's rent, Stephanie told us to come back the next day at noon, and when we arrived, it was almost a different house. They'd found furniture for the rooms, they'd made up the girls' bedroom, they'd cleaned it for us — they'd made it feel like a home. I remember walking into the house and Stephanie was lying on the floor, sweeping under the fridge! She was not a young woman! I can't describe how welcome this made us, how happy we were, how supported we felt as we started our new life. We are still close with Toni and Stephanie today, even though we now live in Ickenham. My children see Stephanie as a grandmother. They have a very special and beautiful relationship together and it's wonderful to see.

THERE HAVE BEEN so many people like the lady from Norway, like Achmed, like Frederike, like Toni, and Stephanie; hundreds of angels all along the way on this journey of mine. In Calais, someone gave us a big comfy chair to sit on on the steps of the church, and a British Pakistani gave us the hotplate to cook on and a pot and a knife — he's a very good friend of mine now. These small things, they don't seem much, but they changed our lives. A Lebanese British man, another great friend now, stopped and asked me, "Are you Syrian? I'm coming back to Calais next week — I hope you make it across in that time — but tell me what you miss the most and I can bring it from the UK." "Syrian coffee!" I said, "I miss Syrian coffee and Syrian bread!" He didn't even wait a week, he came back the next day with a huge van full of cans of chickpeas and fava beans, coffee, bread, vegetables, nuts, chocolate bars, and chips. One of the neighbors near the church left out 12 electrical sockets next to his door every day so we could recharge our phones and not spend 5 euros to sit in a local cafe. At 1pm one of us would put all the cell phones in and come back at 6pm to collect them. Every single day. Other neighbors used to come to us and translate the newspaper for us if there was anything about the refugees in Calais.

Although most of the angels in my life have been strangers, showing kindness to others without even knowing their situation, I am so, so lucky to have angels within my own family too. When we were still in Syria, moving around for our safety, my brother Mohammad took us into his home and helped us out financially when my businesses were destroyed. My sister Rania and brother-in-law Thabet too: they left Syria before we did, but let us stay in their house in Damascus. And when I came to the UK, they opened up their home to me again in Doncaster. Thabet is someone you can depend on. He's almost like a mythical personality, doing good, looking for ways he can support people all the time. I can't thank them all enough for being there when we needed them.

I have so many people to thank for getting me to where I am, so many angels I've met, who arrived when I was at my lowest. Despite the horrors I've seen in the world, that we hear about every day on the news, I know that there is also so much goodness out there. I believe that when you have love in your heart, you will find it in other people's faces. Build love in your heart and you will see it in others around you too.

DATE AND TAHINI
SWEET DIP

This is so delicious, and actually makes the best breakfast! You can make as much as you want and put it in a jar to have every morning or as an evening treat.

TO MAKE

✤ ✤ ✤ ✤ ✤ ✤ ✤ ✤ ✤ ✤ ✤ ✤ ✤ ✤ ✤ ✤ ✤

2 tablespoons date molasses
2 tablespoons tahini
⅓ cup (50 g) toasted sesame
  seeds

Mix the ingredients together in a small bowl and serve with flatbreads or toast.

MAHALABIYA

Mastic gum is a natural tree resin that acts like a gelatin, but with flavor. You can find it online and I really recommend getting hold of it.

TO MAKE

✤ ✤ ✤ ✤ ✤ ✤ ✤ ✤ ✤ ✤ ✤ ✤ ✤ ✤ ✤ ✤ ✤ ✤

4¼ cups (1 liter) whole milk
½ cup (65 g) cornstarch
½ cup (100 g) sugar
2 bay leaves
2 pieces of mastic gum
⅔ cup (150 ml) heavy cream
Scant ½ cup (100 g) condensed milk
2 teaspoons orange blossom water

Pour the milk into a bowl, add the cornstarch and all but 1½ tablespoons of the sugar, then whisk well until the sugar has dissolved.

Now pour the mixture into a large pot over medium-high heat with the bay leaves. Bring to a boil, then turn down to low and simmer for a few minutes until slightly thickened.

Using a mortar and pestle, crush the mastic gum and remaining 1½ tablespoons sugar together until very, very fine (like table salt).

Add the mastic a little at a time to the milk, still over the heat (it's very important it's still hot), whisking as you go, then whisk in the cream, followed by the condensed milk and orange blossom water. Take off the heat and pour into ramekins or glasses.

Allow to cool for 1 hour, then set in the fridge for 6 hours, or ideally overnight.

TO SERVE

✤ ✤ ✤ ✤ ✤ ✤ ✤ ✤ ✤ ✤ ✤ ✤ ✤ ✤ ✤ ✤ ✤

⅔ cup (150 ml) heavy cream, lightly whipped
Candied cherries
Shelled pistachios
Fresh mint
Strawberries or any berries in season
Unsweetened shredded coconut

Serve decorated with lightly whipped cream, candied cherries, pistachios, fresh mint, fruit, or shredded coconut, or any combination.

TAMRIAH

Dates with cookies

MAKES ABOUT 16 SQUARES

It's really important to taste your dates here. Dates from Jordan aren't as sweet as the ones from Iraq or Saudi Arabia.

TO MAKE

❖ ❖ ❖ ❖ ❖ ❖ ❖ ❖ ❖ ❖ ❖ ❖ ❖ ❖ ❖ ❖ ❖

3½ oz (100 g) almonds, cashews, and pistachios (all or just one of these, whichever you like)

½ cup (50 g) walnuts

2 tablespoons ghee

1 lb 7 oz (650 g) medjool dates, pitted and roughly chopped

½ teaspoon ground cardamom

½ teaspoon ground cinnamon

2 teaspoons orange blossom water

5½ oz (150 g) plain Rich Tea or Maria or similar cookies

Preheat the oven to 350°F (180°C).

Toast your nuts on a large baking sheet for 5 minutes until lightly golden, then set aside to cool. Once cool, roughly chop.

Melt the ghee in a medium pot over low heat. Add the chopped dates and stir for a few minutes until the dates have softened into the ghee. Now add the cardamom, cinnamon, and orange blossom water. Stir it all together so it creates a paste — I put on a plastic glove and mash it together with my hand, but you can just get a potato masher or something similar to mix it to a paste.

In a bowl, crush the cookies with your hands into a rough crumble; it's good to have some larger chunks for bite, so don't go too fine. Add to the pot with the date paste.

Line an 8 in (20 cm) square baking pan with parchment paper, then spoon in your chunky date mixture. Even out the mixture to ½ in (1 cm) thick, sprinkle the nuts evenly over the top, then press them into the dates. Set in the fridge for 1 hour, then slice into 16 squares or however many pieces you want.

These will keep for a week in a container out of direct sunlight.

218 **DESSERTS**

BIRD'S NEST

FOR THE NEST

✧ ✧ ✧ ✧ ✧ ✧ ✧ ✧ ✧ ✧ ✧ ✧ ✧ ✧ ✧ ✧ ✧

⅓ cup (40 g) shelled pistachios
10½ oz (300 g) kataifi pastry

Soak the pistachios in water for 30 minutes, then drain.

Cover the kataifi with a damp tea towel so it doesn't dry out as you work. Take a finely twisted 12 in (30 cm) length of pastry and wrap it in a circular motion around two fingers into a nest shape. Transfer to a baking pan, then repeat with the rest of the pastry.

Drain the pistachios and gently press 4 or 5 into the middle of each nest. Cover the nests with a layer of parchment paper, then put a baking sheet on top and put a heavy weight (2 lb 4 oz/1 kg) on top of the paper. Leave at room temperature for 1 hour, then remove the weight, top baking sheet, and paper, and leave for another hour to dry out.

FOR THE SYRUP

✧ ✧ ✧ ✧ ✧ ✧ ✧ ✧ ✧ ✧ ✧ ✧ ✧ ✧ ✧ ✧ ✧

2 cups (400 g) sugar
2 cups (500 ml) water
2 tablespoons lemon juice

Meanwhile, for the syrup, dissolve the sugar in the water in a saucepan over medium heat, bring to a boil, and bubble for 15–20 minutes or until reduced and lightly syrupy. Stir in the lemon juice and boil for a further minute. Remove from the heat and set aside.

TO ASSEMBLE

✧ ✧ ✧ ✧ ✧ ✧ ✧ ✧ ✧ ✧ ✧ ✧ ✧ ✧ ✧ ✧ ✧

1⅔ cups (375 g) butter, melted
  (3 sticks and 2 tablespoons)

Preheat the oven to 425°F (220°C).

Pour the butter over and around the nests, so that they're sitting in a layer of melted butter. Bake for 20–25 minutes until golden brown, turning the pan from time to time to make sure the nests are evenly colored. Leave to cool for 10 minutes, then transfer to a clean baking pan and pour over the syrup. Leave to cool completely in the syrup, then serve.

BESBUSI

FOR THE CAKE

✦ ✦ ✦ ✦ ✦ ✦ ✦ ✦ ✦ ✦ ✦ ✦ ✦ ✦ ✦ ✦ ✦ ✦

1¾ cups (300 g) medium
  semolina
1¾ cups (150 g) unsweetened
  desiccated coconut
½ teaspoon ground cardamom
½ cup (50 g) dried milk powder
1½ teaspoons baking powder
Pinch of salt
3 eggs
¾ cup (150 g) sugar
1½ teaspoons vanilla paste
¾ cup (200 ml) vegetable oil
1¼ cups (300 g) yogurt
Zest of 1 lemon
1 tablespoon tahini
Handful of blanched almonds

Preheat the oven to 350°F (180°C).

In a mixing bowl, put the semolina, desiccated coconut, cardamom, milk powder, baking powder, and salt and mix to combine.

In another bowl, whisk the eggs, sugar, vanilla, vegetable oil, yogurt, and lemon zest together until smooth, then add this to the dry ingredients, mixing until you have a smooth batter.

Grease a 12 x 16 in (30 x 40 cm) baking pan or dish with the tahini then pour in the batter. Smooth out the top with the back of a spoon then tap on a surface to remove any air. Scatter over or arrange the almonds and place on the middle rack of the oven for 30 minutes.

FOR THE SUGAR SYRUP

✦ ✦ ✦ ✦ ✦ ✦ ✦ ✦ ✦ ✦ ✦ ✦ ✦ ✦ ✦ ✦ ✦

Scant ½ cup (100 ml) water
½ cup (100 g) sugar
1 slice of lemon
1½ tablespoons ghee

While the cake is in the oven, put the water and sugar in a small saucepan and slowly bring to a boil. Once boiling, turn down to a simmer for 3 minutes then add in the slice of lemon.

Melt the ghee in the sugar syrup and place over very low heat to keep warm until the cake is ready.

TO FINISH

✦ ✦ ✦ ✦ ✦ ✦ ✦ ✦ ✦ ✦ ✦ ✦ ✦ ✦ ✦ ✦ ✦

Remove the cake from the oven, and immediately pour over two-thirds of the warm syrup. Set the rest of the syrup aside.

Slice into 24 squares then pour over the remaining syrup.

Leave to cool in the pan or dish for 30 minutes and serve warm or cold. Store in an airtight container in a cool dark place for 4 – 5 days.

IBIZA KONAFA

I created this when I was catering in Ibiza in 2018 and 2019 in the Pikes hotel, where I went to cook for the charity Choose Love.

FOR THE FILLING

✤ ✤ ✤ ✤ ✤ ✤ ✤ ✤ ✤ ✤ ✤ ✤ ✤ ✤ ✤ ✤ ✤ ✤

Ghee, for greasing
3½ oz (100 g) mixed nuts
    (use whatever you have—I
    like cashews, walnuts, and
    pistachios)
1 quantity sugar syrup
    (page 222) or agave syrup
½ teaspoon ground cardamom
3 tablespoons heavy cream

Preheat the oven to 400°F (200°C). Grease a 12-hole muffin pan with a little ghee.

Tip the nuts onto a baking sheet and toast in the oven for 5 minutes, then remove and allow to cool before pulsing in a food processor with 2 tablespoons of the sugar syrup and the ground cardamom until you have a rough, sticky crumb. Now add the cream and pulse again until combined.

FOR THE PASTRY

✤ ✤ ✤ ✤ ✤ ✤ ✤ ✤ ✤ ✤ ✤ ✤ ✤ ✤ ✤ ✤ ✤ ✤

7 oz (200 g) kataifi pastry
Scant ½ cup (100 g) ghee
¼ tsp ground cardamom
Generous pinch of
    saffron threads

Crush the pastry into fine pieces in a bowl. Melt the ghee with the cardamom and saffron, then pour over the crushed pastry. Mix with your hands until evenly coated.

Spoon 1 generous tablespoon of the pastry into each muffin hole, using up half the mixture. Press the pastry down with your fingers so it's evenly compressed, then add a tablespoon of the creamy nut filling to each, or until you have used it all up and distributed it evenly. Add the remaining pastry to the tops, pressing it in.

Bake in the oven for 25 minutes until lightly golden and starting to crisp. Meanwhile, heat up the remaining sugar syrup.

Remove the konafa from the oven and immediately pour 1 tablespoon of the hot sugar syrup over each one.

Get a large baking sheet similar in size to the muffin pan, and carefully and quickly flip the hot pan over so the konafa tip out. Allow to cool slightly then serve warm or cold.

WHY SYRIANS FEEL
LEFT BEHIND

RIGHT NOW, EVERYONE I KNOW is trying to escape from Syria. The situation there has never been more desperate. But sometimes I feel as though the world has forgotten Syria, that they've moved on, left us behind. Assad's rule is as harsh as ever, worse than before, but even now they call Hafez al-Assad, Bashar's father, "the immortal commander." Ten hours a day, news cycles on Syrian TV talk about Assad's glory. It just keeps going. One day, surely, it must end, but I can't imagine when or how. I hope I will be alive to see it happen, for my daughters.

I think for many people outside of Syria, especially in Western and European countries, Syria feels too far away, both geographically and in terms of our lifestyle. But we were no different to you. Our lives were the same: we worked, our children went to school, our cities were busy and modern, we enjoyed our social lives, we ran our own businesses, we had all the same dreams for ourselves and our families.

There may not be as many rocket bombs falling each night now, but there is no gas, no electricity, no money left to run the infrastructure to support normal life. In Damascus you get power for a couple of hours each day, but in other cities, in rural areas, it might be an hour a couple of times a week if you're lucky. People work twelve hours a day, but don't have enough to buy the basics. Without the help of friends and family outside of Syria, you cannot get by. But it's so risky to receive that help, the regime would view it as supporting ISIS or bringing down Syria from the inside. It's a dark, dangerous time, with people dying in jails, or disappearing with no hope of being found.

People call it a civil war, but it's not our war anymore. It's a complex battlefield playing out among other nations, while ordinary Syrians can only sit by and watch, powerless. Russia and Iran have launched attacks in support of Assad; ISIS and al-Qaeda have taken advantage of the chaos and taken over vast areas of the country; the USA has conducted air strikes on the Islamic State; Turkey launched its own invasion driving out Kurdish-rules areas; Israel is bombing Hezbollah in Syria every single week. And there are many, many smaller, local rebellion groups, fighting to gain their own slice of power. It's a mess. A mess that has resulted in the death of hundreds of thousands and six million people fleeing the country. When I was in Syria, I was the luckiest one of my neighbors as I lost only businesses, not a member of my family, unlike most of them.

So I am shocked when people don't know where Syria is, when they ask how things are now. Honestly, it makes me angry to see the response to the situation in Ukraine, compared with how the world reacted to what happened in Syria. It feels like there are two classes of refugees: and the difference is to do with the color of our skin. I feel Syrians — and Iranians, and the Sudanese, and so many others – have been failed by governments around the world. We feel betrayed. Hundreds of red lines have been given to Assad, and all of them were crossed, with no repercussions. There are so many good people in the world, I can't tell you how warm the hearts of the UK people are. But their governments are not representing the people. People ask me why we have refugees from Syria here. They don't know it's because their governments didn't do anything to step in and help; they took no action.

Why was it OK for Russia to host the World Cup in 2018 when it was killing people in Syria, but it wasn't acceptable for Russia to compete in the 2022 Olympics because of their attack on Ukraine? I can give you a direct number to the Home Office if you are a Ukrainian refugee, but if you are from any other nation, there is a recorded message to say they can't do anything because they are overwhelmed with assisting Ukrainians. We are all the same, we are all just people, we need to reach out to each other, to listen to each other's stories, to learn from each other.

I have been made to feel so welcome by the people I've met all along my journey. It has rebuilt my faith in humanity, in the innate goodness of people all over the world. But I don't feel like our governments, our leaders, the media are on our side. They are part of the problem, not the solution. There are so many people who are trying so hard to be positive against the whole world, and we need to join together, not make more divisions.

KONAFA NABLUSIYEH

FOR THE SUGAR SYRUP

❖ ❖ ❖ ❖ ❖ ❖ ❖ ❖ ❖ ❖ ❖ ❖ ❖ ❖ ❖ ❖ ❖ ❖ ❖

Scant ½ cup (100 ml) water
½ cup (100 g) sugar
1 slice of lemon

Start with the sugar syrup. Add the water and sugar to a small saucepan and slowly bring to a boil. Once boiling, turn down to a simmer for about 5 minutes then add in the slice of lemon and reduce the heat to the lowest setting while you get everything else ready.

FOR THE KONAFA

❖ ❖ ❖ ❖ ❖ ❖ ❖ ❖ ❖ ❖ ❖ ❖ ❖ ❖ ❖ ❖ ❖ ❖ ❖

7 oz (200 g) tresse cheese, akawi, or any kind of very salty, hard white cheese
Scant ½ cup (100 g) ghee, plus extra for greasing
Few drops of yellow food coloring (optional)
7 oz (200 g) kataifi pastry, chopped into small pieces
2⅔ oz (75 g) mozzarella, grated
Chopped pistachios, to serve

Grate the hard cheese and put it in a bowl of cold water. Then pour out the water and refill again. Repeat this 4 times to get rid of as much salt in the cheese as possible. Drain and put it on a clean, dry tea towel to get as much moisture out as possible.

Melt the ghee in a small pot or in the microwave, then add the yellow coloring, if using. Put the pastry in a bowl with the melted ghee and mix really well so it's all evenly coated.

Brush a 12 in (30 cm) nonstick frying pan with a little more ghee, then add the pastry and press it down firmly into the pan. Now add the grated hard cheese and mozzarella to the middle of the pastry, leaving a ½ in (1.5 cm) border around the edge.

Place over medium-low heat, off-center so the flame or heat sits on the edges and not in the center. We want to crisp up the bottom very lightly but also melt the cheeses on top, so we have to work slowly and carefully. Stand at the stove for about 10 minutes, turning the pan every few seconds so the heat is evenly distributed underneath, until you can see the edges turning golden and the cheese is melted on top.

Get your serving plate, one that is larger than the pan. Put the plate on top of the pan and carefully and confidently flip over so the pastry is face up.

Turn the heat up on the syrup for a minute then, while hot, spoon over a few ladlefuls. You won't need all the syrup, so don't overdo it. Finish with chopped pistachios and serve immediately, while it's hot.

AWWAMA

Donuts in date molasses

This makes a lot, so feel free to halve the recipe.

TO MAKE

✦ ✦ ✦ ✦ ✦ ✦ ✦ ✦ ✦ ✦ ✦ ✦ ✦ ✦ ✦ ✦ ✦ ✦

1½ cups (350 ml) lukewarm water

¼ oz (7 g) envelope fast-acting instant yeast

½ teaspoon ground cardamom

Pinch of kosher or coarse sea salt

Pinch of saffron threads

3⅓ cups (400 g) all-purpose flour

1 tablespoon cornstarch

2 tablespoons agave syrup

½ teaspoon vanilla extract

6⅓ cups (1.5 liters) vegetable oil, plus extra for shaping

Date molasses, to serve

Mix the lukewarm water and yeast together in a jug then set aside for 10 minutes to bubble up.

Using a mortar and pestle, grind the cardamom, salt, and saffron together.

Sift the flour, cornstarch, and cardamom mixture into a stand mixer with the dough hook attached. Mix for a few seconds to combine, then, with the machine running, slowly pour in the yeast and water mixture and the agave syrup and vanilla, until evenly combined and there are no flour pockets left. Turn up to full speed for 5 minutes until the dough is slightly stretchy but still quite wet. Remove the bowl from the mixer, put a tea towel or plastic wrap over the bowl, and set aside to rise for an hour, or until doubled in size.

Pour the vegetable oil into a deep, heavy-based pot and place over medium-high heat until it reaches 340°F/170°C (if you don't have a thermometer, test by adding a little bit of dough to the oil; if it bubbles and rises to the top, you're ready to go).

Once the dough has risen, wet your hands and mix it gently for a few seconds. Place a small bowl of cold vegetable oil next to the stove, for shaping the donuts.

Get the bowl of dough and a teaspoon, then with your hands, grab a handful of the dough and squeeze your hand tightly, until the dough pops out at the top of your fist. Then dip the teaspoon into the cold oil (to prevent the dough from sticking) and scoop the dough that's formed in your hand into it, then drop it into the hot oil. Repeat, dipping the spoon in the cold oil every so often to prevent sticking.

Working in batches, deep-fry for 4–5 minutes until lightly golden, pushing the donuts down in to the oil with a long-handled slotted spoon so they all cook evenly. Remove from the oil using the slotted spoon and transfer to a colander set over a bowl to catch the excess oil. Allow to cool for 10–20 minutes.

We are now going to re-fry them, to give them their distinctive crunchy outer layer. Reheat the oil, but this time to 350°F (180°C). Once hot (again, you can test this by adding some leftover dough to the oil, and if it bubbles and floats faster than last time, you're ready).

In batches, re-fry the donuts for a further 3 minutes until golden. Transfer from the oil onto paper towels, then serve hot, with a generous drizzle of date molasses.

SIX

DRINKS

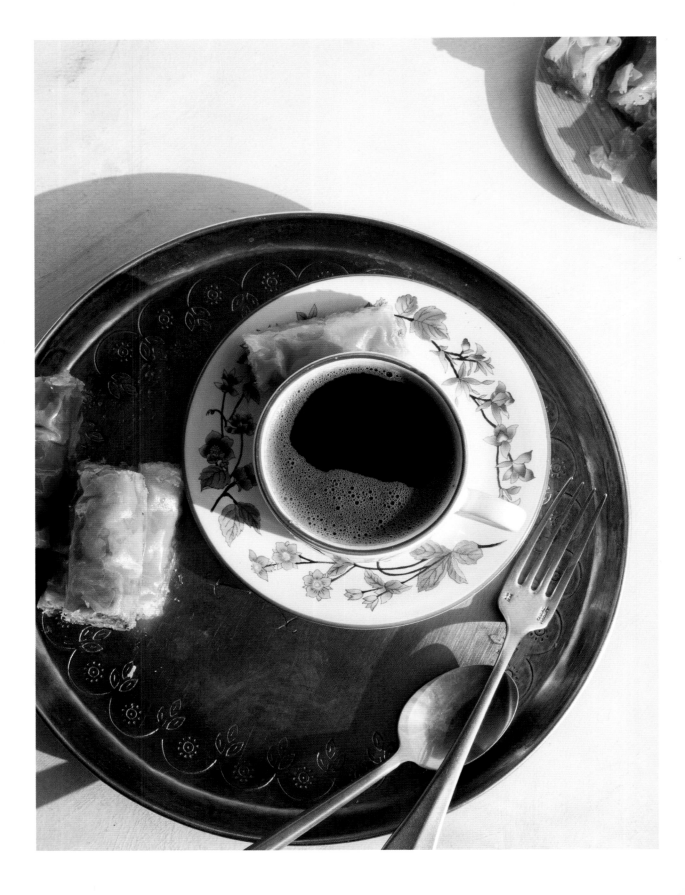

QAWAH

Coffee

In Syria, we have a mixture of 75% medium roast and 25% dark roast in our coffee. We do this ourselves, but you can buy this mix already made in shops.

Pictured left.

SERVES 2

2½ espresso cups of water
2 teaspoons ground coffee (Turkish fine grind)

Pour the water into a Turkish coffee pot and place over medium-high heat. When the water starts to boil, take it off the heat. Give it a few seconds then add the ground coffee. Put it back over the heat until it's boiling again, then take it off to stir (this is so it doesn't boil too fast and burn the coffee). Continue to put it back on and off the heat in this way about 3 times, or until prepared to your liking.

Serve immediately.

TAMARIND JUICE

SERVES 4

2 quantities of tamarind sauce (page 130)
⅔ cup (150 ml) agave syrup or ½ cup (100 g) sugar
1 teaspoon orange blossom water
4¼ cups (1 liter) water
1 lemon, sliced, to serve

Mix together the tamarind sauce (you should have a scant 1 cup/200 g), agave or sugar, orange blossom water, and the water.

Pour over some ice cubes and add a slice of lemon.

Pictured overleaf.

CHAI

Tea

SERVES 2

2 cardamom pods
½ cinnamon stick
1 teaspoon Earl Grey tea leaves
Sugar (optional)

Put the cardamom, cinnamon, and tea in a teapot
and fill with boiling water. Allow to brew for
5 minutes before straining into mugs. Serve with
a little sugar, if you like.

KAMUN

SERVES 2

1 tablespoon cumin seeds
1 lemon

Put the cumin seeds in a teapot and fill with boiling
water. Allow to brew for 5 minutes before straining
into mugs with a squeeze of lemon.

Pictured right.

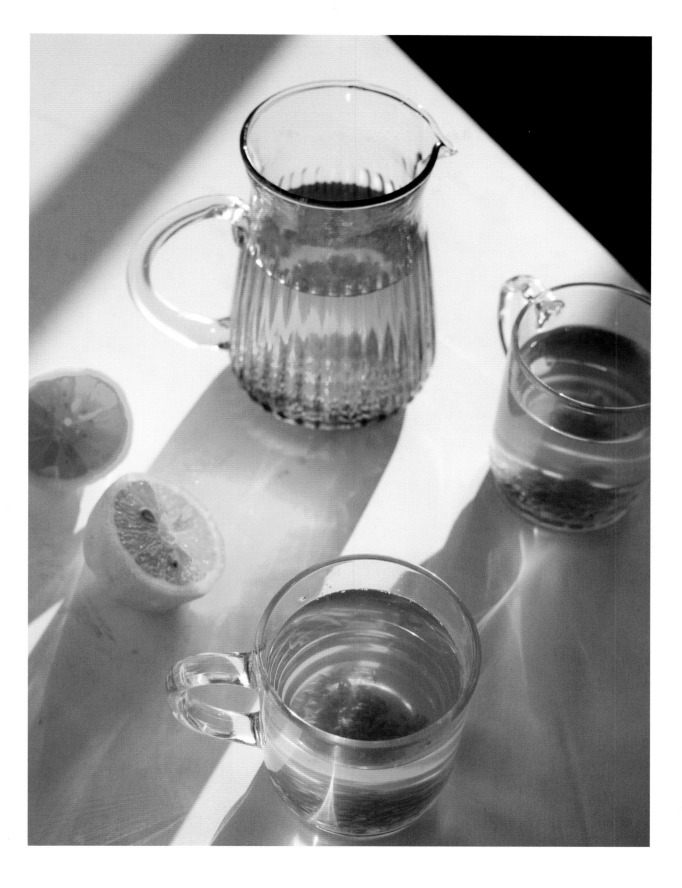

A FINAL MESSAGE

IF THERE'S ONE MESSAGE I want my story to spread, it's to not take what you have for granted because you don't know when it might be taken from you. How many times in our global history do we have to suffer? How many millions have to die or flee their homes to know that our freedom can be removed so quickly, before we learn to protect it? To hold it close and not let it go?

When life is good, we think it will stay like this forever. But look around you. I'm not a politician, I would never want to be one, but even I can see that when you put money and power first, when you put profits and personal gain over protecting people, you are being short-sighted. It's not how you build a great country, it's how you create a temporary win for your party. When you prioritize the people, when you support them, educate them, house them, protect their access to healthcare, you are building a strong nation that will be productive and happy for hundreds of years.

Many people are afraid of refugees, of asylum seekers. Don't be. I'm not saying we are all angels, but not all people are angels either. We are just regular people, forced into situations we never dreamed of. If you want to hear about what it's like to be a refugee, ask them; ask me. I know about these experiences. If you want to know about any minority group, just speak to them. Don't listen to the ugly media that make us all out to be bad people. Being a refugee doesn't mean I am less educated, know less about the world, was less successful. And people don't only flee because of war; they are forced to leave their homes because of earthquakes, floods, droughts. Even here in the UK people are starting to feel the consequences of our changing planet. Refugees are like everyone else around you. Let's respect each other because we are all the same, we are all human beings. We don't know what each other has been through to be here today.

When we listen to the lies of our leaders, their repeated corruption, and do nothing about it, we lose our power, we lose our voice, and often without noticing, bit by bit we lose our liberties. I'm not talking about Syria here; I'm talking about many places. The British people were told life would be better after Brexit, but it is worse. Far worse than before. Who'd have thought our nurses would be relying on foodbanks, that people cannot afford to heat their homes?

We need to raise up our voices. This is the simplest thing you can do. Help as much as you can. Come together on a human level. Search for charities that support people on the ground. Try to make changes where you can, speak to each other, learn from each other. Vote for change if you don't like what you see.

The world is full of amazing, generous people; there is so much love —
I have seen it first-hand! And if we come together, we can achieve miracles.
We need to feel part of the whole world. We need to get rid of the idea
of some people being better than others. We need to listen to each other,
to not be scared of things we don't know, to learn about one another. We
are a global community now. We are not our governments, and we need
to have a voice. You don't know how important your voice is. I don't think
Ukranians thought that this was possible a few years ago, but now they are
refugees. Don't think it can't happen to you. It happened to me, and it can
happen to anyone.

CONVERSION
CHARTS

LIQUID MEASURES

METRIC	IMPERIAL
1.25 ml	¼ tsp
2.5 ml	½ tsp
5 ml	1 tsp
15 ml	1 tbsp
30 ml	1 fl oz (2 tbsp)
50 ml	1¾ fl oz
75 ml	2½ fl oz
100 ml	3½ fl oz
120 ml	4 fl oz
150 ml	5 fl oz
175 ml	6 fl oz
200 ml	6¾ fl oz
250 ml	8½ fl oz
275 ml	9 fl oz
300 ml	10 fl oz
325 ml	11 fl oz
350 ml	12 fl oz
375 ml	12½ fl oz
400 ml	14 fl oz
450 ml	15 fl oz
475 ml	16 fl oz (1 US pint)
500 ml	18 fl oz
600 ml	20 fl oz
700 ml	23 fl oz
850 ml	29 fl oz
1 liter	32 fl oz (1 quart)
1.2 liters	40 fl oz
1.3 liters	44 fl oz
1.4 liters	48 fl oz
1.75 liters	59 fl oz
2 liters	68 fl oz
3 liters	100 fl oz

SPOONS

1 tsp	5 ml
1 tbsp (3 tsp)	15 ml

DRY WEIGHTS

METRIC	IMPERIAL
10 g	⅓ oz
15 g	½ oz
20 g	¾ oz
30 g	1 oz
40 g	1½ oz
50 g	1¾ oz
60 g	2 oz
70 g	2½ oz
75 g	2⅔ oz
100 g	3½ oz
115 g	4 oz
125 g	4½ oz
150 g	5 oz
160 g	5⅔ oz
175 g	6 oz
200 g	7 oz
225 g	8 oz
250 g	9 oz
275 g	9¾ oz
300 g	10½ oz
350 g	12 oz
375 g	13 oz
400 g	14 oz
425 g	15 oz
450 g	16 oz (1 lb)
500 g (0.5 kg)	1 lb 2 oz
550 g	1 lb 4 oz
600 g	1 lb 5 oz
675 g	1 lb 8 oz
725 g	1 lb 10 oz
800 g	1 lb 12 oz
850 g	1 lb 14 oz
900 g	2 lb
1 kg	2 lb 4 oz
1.25 kg	2 lb 12 oz
1.4 kg	3 lb
1.5 kg	3 lb 5 oz
1.6 kg	3 lb 8 oz
1.8 kg	4 lb
2 kg	4 lb 8 oz

INDEX

THANK YOU TO

To my mother and father; my wife, Batool, and my daughters Dana, Lana, and Mariam Alarnab.

Heidi Nam Knudsen

Gemma Bell

Gemma Bell and company

Layla Yarjani

Hortense Decaux

Serena Guen

Josephine Naughton

David and Jenny Edington

Jazz Sherman

Asma khan

Hassan Akkad

A H Alaa

A K Amar

Ross Bailey

Philip Khoury

Melissa Hemsley

Imran Khan and family

Farah Bsieso

Alice Aedy

Jay Rayner

HRH Prince El Hassan bin Talal

Mohammed Khaeir Abukalam

Philli Boyle

Joy Said

Amel Hamza

Simon J Quayle

Elisa Dglv

Toni Broodelle

Gerry Pridham

Sahar Pridham

- Tom Doust
- Vanessa Faulkner
- Marlow Refugee Action
- Wycombe Refugee Partnership
- Emily Madera
- Cassy Paris
- Choose Love
- Appear here
- Saima Khan
- Airbnb
- Kind Snacks
- Clerkenwell Boy
- Dave Burt
- Alice Sampo
- Ahmad Algeria
- Frederique Bougault
- Ahmad Elsidawi
- Kate Walsh
- Saleema Burney
- Tanveer Husain
- Stephanie Rybak
- Thabet Kalthoum
- Daisy Squires
- Mohammad Alarnab
- Rania Alarnab
- The Lady from Norway who I met in Greece

My agent Rachel Mills, the designers at Evi-O.Studio, my editor Laura Bayliss, photographer Andy Sewell, food stylist Kitty Coles, prop stylist Louie Waller, and all those at HQ and HarperCollins.

First published in 2024 by

INTERLINK BOOKS
An imprint of
Interlink Publishing Group, Inc.
46 Crosby Street
Northampton, Massachusetts 01060
www.interlinkbooks.com

Published simultaneously in
Great Britain by HQ, an imprint of
HarperCollinsPublishers Ltd 2023

Library of Congress Cataloging-in-
Publication Data available

ISBN 978-1-62371-116-0

Design and illustration:
Evi-O.Studio | Susan Le
Illustration Assistants:
Evi-O.Studio | Katherine Zhang & Siena Zadro
Typesetting: Evi-O.Studio | Marcus Cheong
Editor: Laura Bayliss
American Ed. Editor: Leyla Moushabeck
Photography: Andy Sewell
Food stylist: Kitty Coles
Prop stylist: Louie Waller
Copyeditor: Sally Somers
Proofreader: Jennifer McKenna
Art Director: Laura Russell
Publishing Director: Louise McKeever
Production: Halema Begum

Printed in Malaysia by Papercraft
10 9 8 7 6 5 4 3 2 1

To browse our full catalog, please visit
www.interlinkbooks.com

FSC
www.fsc.org

MIX
Paper | Supporting
responsible forestry
FSC™ C007454